MARVELLOUS PARTY

Books by Jon Wynne-Tyson include:

THE CIVILIZED ALTERNATIVE
FOOD FOR A FUTURE
SO SAY BANANA BIRD (a novel)
THE EXTENDED CIRCLE (an anthology)

PLAYSCRIPT 116

MARVELLOUS PARTY
A Comedy in Two Acts

Jon Wynne-Tyson

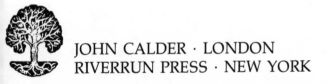

JOHN CALDER · LONDON
RIVERRUN PRESS · NEW YORK

First published in Great Britain, 1989, by
John Calder (Publishers) Limited
18 Brewer Street, London W1R 4AS

and in the United States of America by
Riverrun Press Inc
1170 Broadway, New York, NY10001

British Library Cataloguing in Publication Data

Wynne-Tyson, Jon *1924—*
   Marvellous party. — (Playscript: 116)
   I. Title
   822'.914

   ISBN 0-7145-4178-8

Library of Congress Cataloging-in-Publication Data

Wynne-Tyson, Jon.
   Marvelous party.

   1. Coward, Noël, 1899–1973, in fiction, drama,
poetry, etc.   2. Wynne-Tyson, Esmé, 1898–1972.—Drama.
I. Title.
PR6073.Y73M37   1989   822'.914   88-32197
ISBN 0-7145-4178-9

Printed in Great Britain by Villiers Publications Ltd, London N6 5AH

MARVELLOUS PARTY

Marvellous Party is an entirely imaginary comedy, but based on special knowledge and offering a character assessment of two very real and remarkable people — one a world-famous man of the theatre; the other a woman who retired early from the theatrical limelight to be little known outside the circle that admired her writings and respected her intense desire to help create a more compassionate society. These included Sybil Thorndike, Edith Summerskill, Rebecca West, Richard St Barbe Baker, Radhakrishnan and Vera Brittain.

Noël Coward and Esmé Wynne (1898–1972) were inseparable childhood friends from 1911 when Noël was given a small rôle in *Where the Rainbow Ends* in which Esmé played the lead as Rosamund. Their producer, Charles Hawtrey, that year put on a fairy play by Esmé at the Savoy Theatre. This, and Esmé's already prodigious output of precocious juvenilia, provoked Noël's writing ambition and they began a collaboration in sketches, lyrics, curtain raisers and plays until, two years after her marriage in 1918 to Lynden Tyson, Esmé left the stage (her last rôle was as Faith in *I'll Leave It To You*) and became an impassioned Christian Scientist with her own ideas about the Good Life.*

They continued to meet and correspond until Esmé's death, but Noël never ceased to regret the end of their professional collaboration, for it had been a continuous, mutually stimulating friendship, closer than that of most brothers and sisters. His regret was intensified by Esmé's despatch of a steady stream of her own books and articles, sent in the frail hope of persuading Noël that his disinterest in personal spiritual growth was a failing he would have done well to repair. Philosophy, ethics, humane education and an idealistic feminism had never exactly gripped his imagination.

Marvellous Party reveals how much, and how little, this divergence affected their relationship.

---

* "Esmé's consuming ambition was to become a writer and in this she succeeded, publishing some very well-reviewed novels. She seems to have been a natural writer in the sense that nothing could stop her writing, her pen racing over the pages. This impressed Noël enormously and it is impossible to exaggerate the influence she exerted over him at this time and in the ensuing years. His competitive spirit contributed; not to be outdone, he too started to write and from then on, like Esmé, never stopped writing until he died."

Cole Lesley, Graham Payne and Sheridan Morley:
Noel Coward and His Friends, Weidenfeld & Nicolson, 1979

WHO WAS WHO, 1971 – 1980

WYNNE-TYSON, Dorothy Estelle Esmé; *b* 29 June 1898; *d* of late H. Innes Ripper and Maude Ripper (*née* Pitt); *m* 1918, Wing Comdr Lynden Charles Wynne-Tyson, OBE (decd) (marr. diss.); one *s*. *Educ:* boarding schs, governess, Belgian convent. Actress under stage-name Esmé Wynne from 1909; original Rosamund in Where the Rainbow Ends, 1911; last stage appearance, Faith in Noel Coward's I'll Leave It to You, 1920. *Plays:* first play, The Prince's Bride, prod by Charles Hawtrey at Savoy Theatre, London, when she was 13; Little Lovers, London, 1922; Security, NY, 1929, London, 1932; one-act collaborations with Noel Coward, England and America; curtain-raisers with, and lyrics for, Noel Coward. *Publications:* Security, 1926; Quicksand, 1927; Momus, 1928; Melody, 1929; Incense and Sweet Cane, 1930; Prelude to Peace, 1936; Strange Rival (with J. D. Beresford), 1940; Men in the Same Boat (with J. D. Beresford), 1943; The Riddle of the Tower (with J. D. Beresford), 1944; The Gift (with J. D. Beresford), 1947; The Unity of Being, 1949; This Is Life Eternal, 1951; The Best Years of Their Lives, 1955; Mithras: the Fellow in the Cap, 1958 (rev. edn 1972); The Philosophy of Compassion, 1962; The Dialectics of Diotima, 1970; contribs to many newspapers and jls inc., into the 1930s, Daily Telegraph, Daily Express, Daily Mail, Evening Standard, Punch, Bystander, Queen, Homes and Gardens, Westminster Gazette; later to (Manchester) Guardian; Listener; Hibbert Jl; Contemporary Review; The Aryan Path; Hindustan Times; many books and jls of comparative religion and philosophy; Editor, World Forum, 1961 – 70. Millennium Guild of America Award winner, 1957, 1962. *Address:* c/o Centaur Press Ltd, Fontwell, Sussex.　　　　　　　　　　　　　　　　　[*Died* 17 *Jan.* 1972

COWARD, Sir Noël, Kt 1970; *b* Teddington, 16 Dec. 1899; *s* of late Arthur Coward and Violet Veitch. *Educ:* Chapel Road Sch.; privately. Made first appearance on stage, 1910, and has made many other successful stage appearances in London and New York, also in cabaret in London and Las Vegas. Played King Magnus in The Apple Cart, Haymarket, 1953. FRSL. Hon. DLitt Sussex, 1972. *Plays:* I'll Leave It to You, 1920; The Young Idea, 1921; The Vortex, 1924; Easy Virtue, 1925; Fallen Angels, 1925; Hay Fever, 1925; On with the Dance (revue), 1925; The Queen was in the Parlour, 1926; This was a Man, 1926; The Marquise, 1927; Home Chat, 1927; Sirocco, 1927; This Year of Grace (revue), 1928; Bitter Sweet (operette), 1929; Private Lives, 1930; Cavalcade, 1931; Words and Music (revue), 1932; Design for Living, 1932; Conversation Piece, 1934; Point Valaïne, 1945; To-Night at Eight-Thirty, 1936; Operette, 1938; Blithe Spirit, 1941; Present Laughter, 1942; This Happy Breed, 1943 (written 1939); Sigh No More (revue), 1945; Pacific 1860 (musical play), 1946; Peace In Our Time, 1947; Ace of Clubs (musical play), 1950; Relative Values (play), 1951; Quadrille, 1952; After the Ball (musical play), 1954; South Sea Bubble, 1956; Nude with Violin, 1956; Look After Lulu, 1959; London Morning (ballet), 1959; Waiting in the Wings, 1960; Sail Away (musical play), 1961 (USA), 1962 (Savoy Theatre); The Girl Who Came to Supper (USA), 1963; High Spirits, 1964; A Song at Twilight; Shadows of the Evening; Come into the Garden Maud, 1966. *Films:* In Which We Serve, 1942; This Happy Breed, 1944; Brief Encounter, 1945; Blithe Spirit, 1945; The Astonished Heart, 1950; Around The World in 80 Days, 1957; Our Man in Havana, 1959; Surprise Package, 1960; Bunny Lake is Missing, 1965; Boom, 1968; The Italian Job, 1968. *Publications:* Collected Sketches and Lyrics, 1931; Present Indicative (autobiography), 1937; To Step Aside, 1939; Middle East Diary, 1945; Star Quality (short stories), 1951; Noël Coward Song Book, 1953; Future Indefinite (autobiography), 1954; Pomp and Circumstances (novel), 1960; The Collected Short Stories of Noël Coward, 1962; Pretty Polly Barlow and other stories, 1964; Lyrics of Noël Coward, 1965; Bon Voyage (short stories), 1967; Not Yet the Dodo (verse), 1967. *Address:* Les Avants, sur Montreux, Switzerland. *Clubs:* Athenæum, Garrick.　　　　　　　　　　　　　[*Died* 26 *March* 1973.

Reprinted by kind permission of A & C Black (Publishers) Limited

PREFACE

Many producible, even commercial, plays fail to find a West End or Broadway theatre. The political and less obvious explanations for this are known to many within the profession and may be of small interest to most outside.

Marvellous Party, at this time of writing, has not been produced, although written six years ago. Whatever its ultimate fate may be, I welcome this opportunity to acknowledge my indebtedness to James Roose-Evans that it has at least been written.

Despite mutual friends of long standing, we have not recalled meeting until James's acclaimed production of *84 Charing Cross Road*. As he had some knowledge of my writing, and with his 1963 revival of *Private Lives* in my mind, I put to him the thought of a play about Noël Coward's early life, sending him by way of background a letter I had had published in the Times Literary Supplement. He not only liked the idea, but commissioned me to get on with it. Without that encouragement I might never have bothered.

My first thought had been of a play depicting Noël and Esmé in their youth, with two older actors as their later selves looking on and commenting wryly on the passage of time and the modifications of youthful aspiration. The ever-patient James, with the speed and compassion one might have expected from the issue of a union between Genghis Khan and Florence Nightingale, dismissed this cumbersome vision and suggested I should let the older Noël and Esmé evoke their own past.

To escape the telephone, post, and other crosses of a workaholic life, I took off for a remote corner of the Cevennes, leaving James with tapes made by my mother and recovered from the brother of James Pope-Hennessy after he had been murdered before completing his definitive life of Coward.

When I returned with the play partly drafted and much clearer in my mind, a letter from James was waiting for me. It suggested, shatteringly, that I should work my material into a book rather than a play. The tapes had not been a success. They had given James an unfortunate and partial impression of both the facts and their author. Her spiritual insistencies had jarred. Her intolerance of certain human failings had driven him straight up to the ceiling. I gave immediate priority to a long and fact-balancing letter and sent this to James with the draft of the play's first act. To our mutual relief he reacted with unqualified approval. This spurred me to complete the second act to his and my agent's complete satisfaction. The road ahead seemed straight, broad and sun-lit.

Not a bit of it, of course. *Marvellous Party* went from management to management without finding a home. The excuses seemed flimsy, improbable, sometimes absurd, especially when they capped blush-making praise for qualities that added up to all the ingredients for a successful production. The least implausible rejection was based on a fear that, after a recent poor play about Coward, and a short-lived revival of one of his own plays, the climate was not encouraging. The enthusiasm of some leading actors and writers cut no ice. The dream that it might be put on at the Theatre Royal, Haymarket — which is what that old team Beaumont and Coward might have arranged for it — faded into the uncertainties of a long night.

Marvellous Party has now joined the ranks (not inconsiderable) of plays published ahead of production. Possibly I am being impatient. Some have suggested it would be best to wait for that "climate" to change. But eight or ten years, it is said, can elapse before managements wake up to what they are missing. It can become difficult to shrug off with youthful insouciance the vacuum of a decade.

Others have suggested I should try to analyse the aetiology of my little problem. But the reasons for what some regard as deliberate suppression are complex and perhaps irrelevant. I do not want to add to the already large pool of pettiness in the small world of the theatre by making this the occasion for speculation and accusation.

I have, however, been persuaded that the play should be made available, if only because it attempts to portray Coward as he really was — or as he might actually have behaved and spoken in the somewhat unlikely situation presented. Readers must judge for themselves whether this attempt has been successful, but I would not have committed the play to print had there not been comforting assurances from some of his closest friends that the likeness is convincing.

The credit for this, if true, must go less to the play's author than to my late mother, whose knowledge of Noël's early mind and lifestyle was unique.

In theatrical terms, the main purpose of the play has been to amuse and to give as accurate a picture as possible of how, in middle age, Noël could behave and talk in the company of his most intimate female friend. It is therefore essentially and intentionally a conversation piece, relying upon a minimum of structure. The purpose, it seemed to me, would have been ill served by an elaborate plot with endless comings and goings. Friendship's true hairs are not let down on a station concourse.

Yet that is a half truth. My memories of Noël range from being, as a small boy, farmed out to his manservant and given a boiled egg in the kitchen at Gerald Road, so that he and Esmé could catch up on several months' gossip, to the incongruity of discussing with him childhood threadworm infestation in the idiotically romantic twilight on the verandah of Firefly Hill, Jamaica, our only company the white owl that fluttered like a fat moth before the backdrop of the Blue Mountains and an improbably circular tropical island in the bay below. But my best memory was when Noël gave me tickets to bring Esmé to see him in *The Apple Cart*, after which we went backstage in his beloved Haymarket. There, despite the popping in of Binkie Beaumont, Joyce Grenfell, and many another, Noël and Esmé touchingly and naturally resumed that old intimacy and affection, sandwiched though it was between the rush and gush of an after-the-show dressing room.

When I decided to publish *Marvellous Party* I was advised that it would be an opportunity to write a long biographical introduction about Noël's early life and his relationship with Esmé. Certainly there is not only a lifetime's store of my mother's memories to draw on, but also her copious notes and those tapes (some made to help Sheridan Morley with *A Talent to Amuse*). I toyed with the thought for a long while, but a burning enthusiasm failed to arrive. Perhaps it all seemed a little too akin to the young man from Uckfield writing an earnest document entitled *Mother Knew Noël Coward*. In the end, I decided to let the play stand on its own feet. If it should help to stimulate demand for a biography of Noël's least documented period, the "block" might disappear.

But is there enough to be said to merit such an exercise? The pleasure Noël brought us was in his wit, quickness, lyrics, music, versatility, and dedicated professionalism. Possibly his superficiality is too taken for granted for his life to be examined in anything but theatrical terms.

Yet there was more to Noël than that, especially in his early years. That the superficiality won — that he consciously crushed another "side" to his nature when he saw how materially and professionally successful he could be by developing his undoubted surface talents — may be deemed a pity by the serious-minded. It was certainly so deemed by Esmé, who never let him forget it, as the play shows. But he brought much joy to millions, for all that he did little to touch their hearts or minds with life's eternal truths. It is no bad thing to be able to make others sing and laugh in this rough and ugly world. It may not "save" it, but it makes it a lot more bearable while we hang around for Doomsday. Even Esmé would have admitted that.

JW-T

PRODUCTION NOTE

The setting of *Marvellous Party* is not wholly fictional. Coward was, of course, in Las Vegas in the 1950s, and his success there was a turning point in "dad's renaissance". As the play makes clear, the greatest improbability is that Esmé would have come within a thousand miles of the place. It heightens the absurdity and vulnerability of the situation in which the play places her.

It is important that portrayers of Noël and Esmé should try to show them as they were. "Interpretation" should strive for imitation, for it is in what they were both really like — out of their respective limelights — that the interest lies. Those who act their parts should soak in the text and subtext of *Marvellous Party*. As background reading, *Present Indicative*, if wildly inaccurate in numerous details, probably comes closest to showing the man behind the public image. Anyone wanting to understand the more complex character of Esmé would do better to study her more demanding later books than the earlier plays, fiction and journalism.

To those who did not know them (and almost no one is still alive who knew both of them well), their ability to quarrel violently one moment and behave quite normally the next may be difficult to accept unless it is understood that their early relationship had been that of an unusually close brother and sister. Although Esmé matured in character, values and intellectual pursuits, Noël changed hardly at all until his dying day. Yet Esmé could return to childhood when in his company, showing herself as responsive as ever to a sense of humour which, as she once said, "made you begin to wobble even before he had said anything."

As I have indicated, because I have tried to show Noël and Esmé as themselves, *Marvellous Party* is, intentionally, more of a character study and conversation piece than a play with a strong dramatic scaffold. Act One is basically a duologue of remembrance. If wished, it could stand by itself. For maximum impact the play needs, as James Roose-Evans wrote, "two brilliant performers" to create a "marvellous sparring/ spurring match which releases the emotional shocks and surprises . . . Everything depends upon superb timing of two highly skilled performers." If Act Two has more structure, it may also be found to carry a more demanding subtext. Noel Willman, hoping to direct the play in New York, wrote that the producers he had shown it to had asked "Who is to play these giant parts? It needs dazzling actors."

As has already been hinted at, it has not been for lack of willing and dazzling actors that no management has so far been found. I hope that amateur and repertory companies will not be dissuaded by the need for excellence from "having a go". Some have said that the dialogue can "hold its own" and that a considered attempt to portray Coward as he was must be not only a challenge to the serious actor, but of considerable interest to students of the history of the British theatre. I hope they are right, but then I am just the author. The only certainty I feel is that the players who can get into the skins of Noël and Esmé will confound those tardy managements.

Faith

From
'I'll Leave It To You',
New Theatre, 21.7.1920

Words by ESMÉ WYNNE
Music by NOEL COWARD

Tell me

Adapted by MICHAEL WALSH

Cast in order of appearance:

GARY, a young actor manqué

BELLBOY

SUELLA, a nurse

NOËL COWARD

ESMÉ WYNNE-TYSON

WAITER

ENGINEER

AUBREY CARRUTHERS

PATTI LOGAN, his wife

MABEL THRIFT, a newspaper reporter

The part of SUELLA can double with MABEL THRIFT; that of the BELLBOY (or the WAITER) with the ENGINEER.

The part of the ENGINEER leaves much to the director's discretion.

The cast's wardrobe will be largely dictated by the styles of the period, but Esmé Wynne-Tyson, while making some concession to fashion, always chose what suited her. On this occasion she might have worn a pretty floral dress made of chiffon or some other 'floaty' material, predominantly pink or pastel blue, perhaps with grey or mauve accessories. Her jewellery was unostentatious — often a cameo and wedding ring, and a string of pearls or simple beads. Her hair, which had begun to grey by the 1950s, was worn fairly short, softly curled to frame her face. Her use of make-up was skilful and restrained. Her skin being pale, she used rouge, but also powder to give the impression of having a natural peaches-and-cream complexion. Her lipstick was never more than a 'touch', and in light colours. She occasionally used nail varnish, but only 'natural'. At no time did she try to look younger than her age, but the effect was always charmingly simple, and above all pretty with soft colours.

ACT ONE

An expensive Las Vegas hotel suite in the mid-1950s. Late afternoon.

Back centre the door from the hotel landing is seen through an arch which forms a small lobby. Left centre is a door to the main bedroom; just beyond it, a drinks cupboard, then a window with an air conditioning unit below. Up left of arch is a piano. Up right, a door to second bedroom. Centre right a mantle above a lavish flower arrangement. For the rest, the furnishings are what might be expected. There should be at least one couch and two easy chairs, and in corner to right of arch a television set. Either side of the arch and on all available surfaces are expensive cellophaned and arranged flowers and other tributes, also a man-sized mauve teddy bear of superior, even rapacious, mien, its arms outstretched. Telegrams and letters are propped on the mantel, etc. Some balloons hang from one of the bear's arms and he wears a party hat. The general feel of the room is one of congratulation and success. No one is on stage when the curtain rises.

When the audience has had time to take in the glamour, from the bedroom left comes uninhibited gargling, spitting, and noises suggesting the clearing of nasal passages. The door bell rings. From the bedroom up right a good-looking, rather gangling young man walks slowly to the door, reading telegrams. He opens door and we see another huge cellophaned sheaf of flowers and the BELLBOY'S legs.

BB	(*laconically*) Can you believe? For Mr Coward!
GARY	(*abstractedly, gesturing*) Fine! O.K.! Great! Where you can.
BB	(*entering*) Jeez, it's hot in here!
GARY	The god-damned air conditioning's on the blink.
BB	I'll tell 'em. (*he points to the card attached to the flowers*) This one's from Cole Porter. The message is real cute.
GARY	O.K., so you want to smell 'em too?

BB   I gotten another. (*holds up small bunch of violets*) ''From Aunty
          Clara with love.'' For Mr Cole Lesley. That right?

GARY   Sure! Mr Coward's secretary. Right now he's five floors down.
          Got a bug Mr Coward can do without. We'll take it.

The BELLBOY *finds an empty space, puts down the flowers, hesitates
hopefully, sees there is going to be no tip, grimaces resignedly, and
exits.* GARY *wanders back to his bedroom. Door bell rings.* GARY *re-
emerges and, still reading, opens door without looking at the visitor
who is a pretty young woman in a trim nurse's uniform.*

          Fine! O.K.! . . .

SUELLA   Hi!

GARY   (*looking round door and switching on the charm*) Oh, hi, gorgeous!
          Thought you were another old bunch of lilies.

SUELLA   (*entering*) Hey, it's like it was the Caribbean in here.

GARY   Our conditioning's packed in. How's *your* little problem?

SUELLA   If you mean Mr Cole, he wants his yellow pyjamas. How's
          yours?

GARY   Which one?

SUELLA   Do you have more than one?

GARY   You know I have. Him in there, and the sexiest girl in Vegas.

SUELLA   (*pleased*) Oh, come *on*!

GARY *pins her to the wall with somewhat overdone passion.*

GARY   Just one little kiss to give me strength for the night ahead.

SUELLA   You're a case, Gary. You know that?

GARY   (*theatrically*) Suella, cherie, I know only you are forever in my
          dreams.

*He is about to kiss her when a second bout of gargling and hoicking
is heard. Suella freezes, then giggles.*

          (*breaking away*) Oh, for Pete's sake! Go get Coley's
          slumberware.

SUELLA *enters bedroom up right.* GARY *returns to reading telegrams.*
SUELLA *re-enters with pyjamas.* GARY *hands her violets.*

Better take these. *Somebody* loves him.

SUELLA   See you, then.

GARY   See you. Round seven?

SUELLA   Round seven. (*blows him a kiss*)

GARY *opens door for her and makes a kiss in her direction as she exits. He wanders centre stage, studying the telegrams, his face registering his reactions.*

GARY   (*reading*) ''Darling, no stupid little bug can spoil your great great triumph.''

From the bedroom left comes the sound of a W.C. being flushed. GARY continues to read.

NOËL   (*off*) *What* was that, dear boy?

GARY   (*returning to previous telegram*) ''Darling, no stupid little bug can spoil your great great triumph.''

NOËL   Your reassurance is most warming.

GARY   It's from Zsa Zsa Gabor.

NOËL   That seems marginally more probable. Give it to her teddy to look after.

GARY *tucks telegram under bear's arm.*

GARY   David Niven's is cute.

NOËL   David is cute.

GARY   He sure dug your party.

NOËL   They all dug my party.

GARY   You must do it three times.

NOËL   Do what?

GARY   Gargle. With each powder in turn. Three times, three times a day.

NOËL   Dear boy, if I gargle any more I shall see my poor, weary throat-lining slip down the wastepipe.

GARY   Coley said to tell you it was vital. He'll get mad.

NOËL   God forbid!

GARY   He sure does rule you with a rod of iron.

NOËL   Not rules. Cocoons. I miss him terribly.

GARY   (*with petulant lift of one shoulder*) It's tough trying to follow an established act.

NOËL *enters in dressing gown over vest and trousers. He is doing some rather strange neck and shoulder exercises, rotating his head, rubbing his throat, etc.*

NOËL   (*with great sincerity*) My dear, dear Gary, you are doing the very best of which you are capable.

GARY   I'd sure like to prove that to you, Mr Coward.

NOËL   (*raising a finger*) As I've told you, I'm not casting for anything just now, and when I do . . .

GARY   I know — it'll be from your friends.

NOËL   (*firmly*) It will be in London. (*he examines cards on the flowers*)

GARY   I could get over.

NOËL   How odd of Marlene to send deep purple what's-their-names. Positively funereal.

GARY   Vivien Leigh's sent forget-me-nots.

NOËL   Quite unnecessary. (*he strokes his neck with both hands*) Really! I could have taken a sharp attack of syphilis in my stride, but of *all* the times to get a throat infection . . .

GARY   Everyone's getting it.

NOËL   That, Gary, is small comfort. Everyone is not expected to achieve vocal magic twice nightly at the Desert Inn. Thank God it's come so near the end of my engagement.

The 'phone rings. GARY *answers it. He holds the receiver out to* NOËL, *who is mopping his forehead.*

GARY   Frank Sinatra.

NOËL   In a civilized country one can open a window.

GARY   I'm on to it. It's your unit.

NOËL   (*taking receiver*) Frankie, you dear old thing, sending those perfectly adorable flowers — and on top of your splendid numbers at my little party. How on earth did you track down such very English roses in the middle of a roasting desert? . . . Well, that was very very extravagant and very very sweet. . . . Oh, a bit croaky if I raise my voice or get over-excited, but dear Alfie's exercises are working a treat and I gargle with such dedication that half the hotel's guests have checked

out . . . No, I don't *think* there have been any garlands from
Judy, but it's the thought that counts. I've had a tiny bunch
of some rather prickly plant from Rita. I don't think she's
forgiven me properly for saying she was a little spotty. I hear
she's caught the virus too, so I'll send her a vast display of
bouganvillea and frangipani to riddle her with remorse . . .
Please do, Frankie darling. I'm confined to barracks for another
evening, but if this idiot bug can be chased off I shall give my
last two performances tomorrow and return to London the
next day . . . You're a duck. My devoted thanks — and love.
(*he replaces receiver as door bell rings*)

GARY   What's it like when things really hot up? (*he opens door. It is
two more bunches of flowers*) Over there, I guess. (*he points to
table down right*)

The BELLBOY *sees* NOËL, *starts to whistle "I'll See You Again" with
an expertise that makes* NOËL *cringe, and exits slowly, his whistle
petering out in a half raspberry at the door when he realizes no tip
is forthcoming*

(*reading label*) Sammy Davis.

NOËL   Bless his tiny cotton socks. I hope his message is not as rude
as Jack Benny's. (*'phone rings*) I'll take it. (*he does so*) Tallulah,
my angel, those *lovely* flowers . . . Oh, didn't you? Well, I'll
bet you intended to, so let me thank you in advance . . . Yes,
it's exactly like sitting all day long in the middle of Covent
Garden. Thank God I don't suffer from hay fever . . . That
was quite witty, darling, so for once I forgive you . . . Yes,
she did. An absolutely vast sheaf of the most gorgeous lilies
that must have cost a small fortune. Am I unique in receiving
more flowers at the end of a run than for the first night?
. . . That was even more unkind, darling. I am an invalid and
should be cherished and soothed . . . Oh, a slow uphill
climb . . . Yes, we most certainly must, but I'm not sure
there's going to be a moment in which to see anyone before
I whizz back to England . . . Darling, please do. If this silly
old virus gets bored with me in time I want to have a small

farewell do in the Sky Room, and it would be a non-event without you . . . Bless you, dear. 'Bye for now. (*replaces receiver*) My *God*, it's exhausting being loved.

GARY   (*tartly*) You've only gargled twice.

NOËL   You're as persistent as Coley. Now if dear old Stoj was here she'd say it was just error and tell it to go away.

GARY   Dear old who?

NOËL   Stoj. My oldest and most exasperating friend. You obviously haven't read my autobiography. Why is your generation so indifferent to the classics?

GARY   We're too busy trying to make it against the competition. Why'd she call it ''error''?

NOËL   She's a rabid Christian Scientist — or was, before she went several stages beyond and above Mary Baker Eddy.

GARY   Oh, sure, my aunty was that way. She got mad at me when I told her that limerick — you know (*recites*):

There was a young man called O'Neill
Who said, ''Although pain isn't real,
When I sit on a pin
And it punctures my skin
I dislike what I *fancy* I feel.''

NOËL   Precisely. Well, all illness is ''error'' to Stoj. Come to think of it, more or less everything is error to Stoj.

GARY   Well, she's not here and you'd best gargle.

The 'phone rings. GARY *answers it.*

And Suella said to tell you not to forget your antibiotic. (*into phone*) Mr Coward's suite. (*to* NOËL) It's the desk. There's an Esmé Wynne-Tyson to see you.

NOËL   An Esmé . . . (*stops rubbing*) Now don't play silly games, dear boy; I am far too frail.

GARY   (*shrugging*) That's what the guy says.

NOËL   But Esmé . . . Stoj . . . is the one I've just been telling you about. She wouldn't have come within five thousand miles of Las Vegas.

GARY   Life's full of surprises.

NOËL   It's either that monstrous matron from Memphis . . .

GARY   Last time she rang she said she was out of town until this
          evening.

NOËL   It nearly is evening. Then it's that reporter on the What's-it-
          Courier again. She's insatiable. Two hours of talking about
          nothing but her Electra Complex. I had no idea how much
          time people spent wallowing in penis envy. I told her never
          again. (*gestures*) It's a trick. Tell them to send her away.

GARY   (*into 'phone*) Mr Coward says to tell the person to scram.
          (*replaces receiver*)

NOËL   (*short laugh*) Stoj! She's as likely to be in Vegas as I am to be
          taking a confessional in St Peter's.

GARY   So old friends turn up now and then.

NOËL   Not Stoj. She doesn't go anywhere. She lives on half a peanut
          and a lettuce leaf in a small timber bungalow, hammering away
          at her typewriter day in, day out, year after year, seeing no
          one. She's like an excessively reclusive Gibbon.

GARY   If her looks are that bad, maybe that's why she doesn't want
          to be seen around.

NOËL   Not *that* kind of gibbon, you fathead! Edward. The writer.
          Decline and Fall. Never stopped scribbling. Stoj is the same.
          She believes a second spent not writing is a second
          squandered.

GARY   They do say you're not exactly into the leisure scene yourself.

NOËL   It's a matter of balance, Gary. I'm not incessantly trying to
          give the world a message. (*shrugs*) Let's face it, I'm not trying
          to give them a message at all. They'd loathe it. I live *in* the
          world, not in judgment of it.

GARY   (*looking at watch*) Listen, I'm losing you and I've really got to go.

NOËL   Stoj has spent the bulk of her life trying to nag the world into
          being better than it wants to be.

GARY   She's a preacher?

NOËL   She writes books. My God, how she writes books! Every one
          a *sledge*-hammer.

GARY   Kind of moral stuff?

NOËL   Prohibitive. She is passionately against almost everything to

	do with human life — drink, sex, smoking, eating meat . . . you name it.
GARY	And she's your oldest pal?
NOËL	We met as children. We were both trained by Charles Hawtrey. She was a quite different cup of tea then. Full of fun and ideas. All right, she had suffered religious spasms from the age of six and could be a bit pompous, which is why I called her Stodge, but . . .
GARY	You went different ways?
NOËL	We certainly did. She gave up the stage and married. Terrible mistake. Turned the religious thing into an obsession.
GARY	It maybe meant more to her.
NOËL	(*nostalgically*) I often think of those early years. More now than before, maybe. Wonderful days. Finding our feet, talking and arguing incessantly, never apart. We worked together, of course — songs, lyrics, curtain raisers, on tour. I put music to her songs and wrote parts for her. I was madly jealous of her at first. She was a splendid little actress, destined for the top. (*almost angrily*) What a waste! One of the lousiest things about getting older, Gary, is learning how people can change.
GARY	Have *you*? Changed?
NOËL	Not if I could help it. But we change in our view of others; in our faith in their ability to stay the course, whether in work or love; in our expectations. People can be an awful let-down, Gary. (*removes dressing gown and puts on shirt*) Damn! Now I've lost a button.
GARY	(*producing needle and cotton*) That's maybe why some of them look for something else. My *aunty* wasn't that impressed by the way the world's shaping up. You're supposed to be resting, not dressing.
NOËL	If you've got to rush off and leave me alone, I must be dressed. Without Coley I'm as defenceless as a shelled snail.

The 'phone rings. NOËL *answers it, adopting a deep butch voice.*

Mr Coward's suite . . . This is Mr Coward's personal bodyguard. Mr Coward is not available, is not giving interviews, and will vigorously challenge the hotel's account unless he is protected from uninvited journalists. (*replaces receiver*)

GARY   (*sewing on button while* NOËL *rotates head*) One of these days it will be Louella Parsons. Mind, or I'll prick you.

NOËL   Louella Parsons is another matter. Even Hedda Hopper is another matter.

GARY   (*severing cotton*) Well, if that's all . . .

NOËL   (*resigned*) Cut along, dear boy. I shall manage somehow. God! How I hate being alone in hotels. Or anywhere, for that matter.

Gary hands him tie, which he puts on.

When Stoj and I were on tour in *Charley's Aunt* we nearly went ga-ga in our separate digs. *I* did, anyway. Not a soul to talk to.

GARY   You could have visited with each other.

NOËL   My dear Gary, it was an old old company that had been going the rounds for decades. They were mostly geriatrics who had grown into their parts. They were incapable of understanding a platonic friendship, so because Stoj wore a skirt and I trousers, we couldn't share digs or even enter each other's room. I have detested being alone from that day to this.

GARY   (*making for the door*) Listen, I'll get them to send up that bottle of Scotch. (*he points to empty decanter*)

NOËL   You mean well, dear boy.

GARY *exits.*

NOËL *walks towards his bedroom, coming face to face with the bear. He studies it for a moment.*

One of us may have to go.

He turns and looks at himself in the mirror. He pushes up his cheeks, smooths his thinning hair, and pinches his neck.

(*as though stating an article of faith*) It *is not you*. It never was and never can be you.

The 'phone rings. He goes to it eagerly.

Hullo, yes? The Coward penthouse . . . Oh, not again! . . . (*doubt showing*) But you can't be Stoj! Stoj in Las Vegas is an unthinkable contradiction . . . Well, yes . . . All right, I agree you do *sound* like her . . . You're what? Three floors down? This is ridiculous! . . . Very well, then, come up. But I warn you, I have a virus and it is very very catching . . . Well, of course it's catching! How do you think *I* got it? . . . Well, bugger Mrs Eddy. (*replaces receiver; his mouth drops*) My God! It *must* be Stoj!

He takes and lights a cigarette from the box on the table, briefly strikes a typical Coward attitude, then quickly stubs the cigarette, flaps at the smoke, circles the room seeking a home for the stub, then enters bathroom and flushes it. He hides the empty decanter in cupboard. Door bell rings. NOËL *puts on dressing gown and makes rapid adjustments at mirror before opening door and standing back warily. The woman who enters briskly is in her mid-50s, small, with grey hair and a lovely complexion. She has poise and charm.*

(*opening arms wide*) Stoj! My dearest Stoj! This is just a dream. It is simply not happening.

ESMÉ	Poj, darling! It's been like getting an audience with the Queen Mum. (*they embrace with theatrical but evident affection*)
NOËL	(*holding her at arms' length*) The Queen Mum is far more accessible.
ESMÉ	You haven't changed an iota.
NOËL	(*guardedly*) Since when?
ESMÉ	That lunch in Gerald Road.
NOËL	Nor you. Not by a wrinkle. God! It was six years ago.
ESMÉ	Seven. It seems yesterday.
NOËL	And now here you are in Vegas. Of all the places for a reunion.
ESMÉ	It's a long story.
NOËL	The night's ahead of us. I've been stuck for three interminable days in this damned bloody awful suite . . .
ESMÉ	Darling, I'm exhausted . . .
NOËL	Let me get you a stiff . . . chair (*gestures*) Can I provide . . . anything?

ESMÉ	(*sitting, thankfully*) Ten minutes' escape from that (*gestures*) . . . that nightmare out there would be absolute bliss. Darling, wouldn't it be an idea to open a window?
NOËL	They don't let you do that sort of thing in America. They are terribly security conscious.
ESMÉ	I don't know how you bear it.
NOËL	Yes, I must say, although Vegas has been a marvellous party, I do rather look forward to getting back to London and my little family.
ESMÉ	Your nice Coley. I gather he's here too. And Graham?
NOËL	No, Graham's keeping the home fires burning.
ESMÉ	I don't think I've ever met him.
NOËL	I think of them both a great deal. Especially in a place like this that is somehow not quite real and just a little frightening.
ESMÉ	''A little frightening'' is the understatement of all time. I should never have left Sussex. I long to get back to the peace and sanity of my study.
NOËL	Calm down, lovie, and tell me every single thing.
ESMÉ	Darling, that would take six years. Seven.
NOËL	But Stoj, my pet, Las Vegas . . .
ESMÉ	(*crossly*) It's Geoffrey, Sir Geoffrey Swale, that publisher of mine.
NOËL	I thought you had him eating out of your hand, like everyone else.
ESMÉ	I'd sooner trust my hand to a sabre-toothed tiger.
NOËL	Well, he publishes your books. It amounts to the same thing. (*'phone rings.* NOËL *answers it*) Coward pent . . . Well, thank God for that. It's like living in an oven. Yes, as soon as you can.
ESMÉ	That's just it. He has begun to impose conditions.
NOËL	Publishers are so terribly commercial these days. They actually expect you to make them money.
ESMÉ	(*sharply*) I *have* made him money. My books have an intensely faithful following. What is more, I have lifted the tone of his list immeasurably. It was full of . . . (*gestures*) well . . . most worldly things.
NOËL	(*pacifically*) Of course, darling, but why Vegas?
ESMÉ	He insisted I do a lecture tour. Otherwise he was going to be difficult about my next book.

NOËL	Lecturing? On what?
ESMÉ	Uplift. What else?
NOËL	Uplift? But no one worries about that any more. It's all done with sponge rubber.
ESMÉ	(*amused*) *Spiritual* uplift.
NOËL	Silly me. (*he picks his nose*)
ESMÉ	Darling! Are you *still* doing that?
NOËL	Doing what?
ESMÉ	Picking your nose.
NOËL	It's infinitely cheaper than cigarettes.
ESMÉ	And no prettier. Anyway, this lecturing business is desperately tiring. They make me tinker with each talk to suit the area.
NOËL	Sort of . . . regional recipes.
ESMÉ	Urgently needed, believe me.
NOËL	So how are you socking it to them in Vegas?
ESMÉ	My dear, the *gambling* in this place . . .
NOËL	Very rife, one hears.
ESMÉ	(*darkly*) And not only gambling. (*she rises*) What heavenly flowers! (*she examines one of the cards*) Dear Edna Best does hold on wonderfully, doesn't she?
NOËL	But you can't just nag . . . talk to them about gambling. It's their major industry. Their bairns would be on dry crusts without the gambling.
NOËL	Orson says I have the faculty for finding common ground with everyone.
NOËL	Orson? I thought you were lecturing, not making a film.
ESMÉ	Orson Humdinger, my . . . well, I suppose you'd call him a tour manager.
NOËL	Darling, not even in America could anyone be Orson Humdinger.
ESMÉ	It rather suits him. He's larger than life, frightfully fit, and seventy-five; but I suppose he has sex appeal if one goes for that kind of thing.
NOËL	An awful lot of us do.
ESMÉ	His own spiritual orientation is another matter. He is far more interested in the takings than the giving. You wouldn't believe it, but he actually tried to get me to take part in some terrible

revivalist jamboree being held this evening in some vast
stadium. A sect that sounds like a cat . . .

NOËL   (*laughing*) Darling! Not the Tabitha Tabernacle! I don't think
that would be you at all. They get sloshed to the gills, sing
sizzling hymns, and quite frequently end up having group sex.
I think you would have to work very very hard to bring them
to Mrs Eddy.

ESMÉ   I do not intend to try. Orson must have been out of his mind.

NOËL   It would pay well, mind. They get national TV coverage.

ESMÉ   (*grimly*) I have no doubt that that was what Orson was bank-
ing on.

NOËL   So you've come to see me instead. That was sweet of you.

ESMÉ   I mustn't be too long. Orson is sending a car to pick me up.
As I said no to the Tabitha thing I agreed to talk to quite a
small group of Quakers instead.

NOËL   You're as rangey as you ever were, darling.

ESMÉ   I hear you've been wonderfully received. (*reading card*)
Humphrey Bogart. What dreadful names people do give
themselves these days.

NOËL   (*modestly*) Yes, yes, they're being awfully kind. I think it's the
Englishness they respond to.

ESMÉ   What a nuisance about this silly virus you think you have
picked up. You must unsee it.

NOËL   I have, darling. Vigorously. Unfortunately it refuses to unsee
me. Vegas is a terrible place to play at the best of times; the
altitude and dryness absolutely feed on the throat lining. Mad-
dening! I had never sung better until the damned virus decided
my larynx was home sweet home. But I've been doing exercises from a wonderful man called Alf Dixon. You make a kind
of moo, up and down the scale, with your lips closed until
your breath gives out.

ESMÉ   I should think *that* is what you are suffering from. ''Virus''
is just another name for error.

NOËL   Now, darling, don't be a contradictory old Stojkins. I quite
definitely have a virus. They can prove it with swabs.

ESMÉ   The material senses tell us all sorts of nonsense.

NOËL   (*tetchily*) It's going the rounds. It's terribly infectious and can take effect almost immediately.

ESMÉ   Darling, everything that is in the mind takes immediate effect. That's why it is so important to fill it only with . . .

Door bell rings.

NOËL   Come! (WAITER *enters with whisky bottle*) Oh! I hoped you were the air conditioning. (*indicates drinks cupboard*) There, please. (*to* ESMÉ) Still the old props, I fear. I *know* I should have grown out of them.

ESMÉ   We all need something, my poor pet. (*her tone suggests it is not alcohol*)

WAITER (*he is a gloomy man*)It's your unit. (*he kicks it*) That can do it. Anything for the lady?

NOËL   No, absolutely nothing. Well . . . (*to* ESMÉ) there must be *something* you would like?

ESMÉ   I'm quite all right, thank you.

NOËL   How about a tuna sandwich?

ESMÉ   Most certainly *not* a tuna sandwich. Have you forgotten that letter you wrote, horrified by the barbaric killing of the poor creatures that you'd witnessed in the West Indies?

NOËL   (*sincerely*) It *was* horrible. Utterly beastly.

ESMÉ   (*she sits*) But it didn't stop you eating them.

NOËL   (*recovered*) There you are quite wrong. For six months I could barely look a *kipper* in the face.

ESMÉ   I'd like an orange juice, made of real oranges. They were the very best thing about California.

NOËL   Of course! Citron pressé! (*to* WAITER) A huge orange juice made of huge, real oranges. With masses of ice.

WAITER You too, Mr Coward?

NOËL   (*waving him to door*) Don't be ludicrous, there's a good fellow. (WAITER *exits*)

ESMÉ   (*magnanimously*) You must have what you have convinced yourself you need.

NOËL   (*sighing*) A tall order! (*he sits in chair opposite* ESMÉ)

ESMÉ   It's marvellous you've made such a comeback.

NOËL   Well, Naples wasn't rebuilt in a day, but I do think dad's renaissance may be on the horizon.

ESMÉ   (*seriously*) I was thinking as I came up in the lift — in our different ways we have *both* demonstrated.

NOËL   Demonstrated? I'm au fait with error and uplift and the jolly old divine Mind, but . . .

ESMÉ   Exactly. The power of Mind. That's what we have both demonstrated.

NOËL   (*sincerely*) Yes. Yes, we have. I was telling Gary much the same before you popped up.

ESMÉ   Gary?

NOËL   He's looking after me, in his fashion. Coley's down with the same damn virus and has capped it with some sort of flu. He's five floors down in the charge of an absurdly expensive nurse.

ESMÉ   (*leaning her head back and gazing at ceiling*) Do you remember — so long, long ago, before I married Lynden, when you and I were so idiotically young — that day when we stood in a field during that awful *Charley's Aunt* tour, when we both knew — absolutely knew, deep down inside — that we could do anything we put our minds to?

NOËL   Of course I remember. We were a very determined young couple.

ESMÉ   It wasn't just determination.

NOËL   It was, you know. Raw, naked ambition.

ESMÉ   In your case it was sheer will power. You wanted the world at your feet, and you succeeded.

NOËL   Precisely. So . . .

ESMÉ   What *I* had was an overwhelming longing to know what life was all about. It wasn't determination because I didn't know *how*. There was obviously no material profit in finding out.

NOËL   You've still had them rolling in the aisles — in your fashion.

ESMÉ   So few of them really want to *know*, or have shared that longing for the Truth.

NOËL   A big girl like you should have twigged by now that Bertie Russell hit the nail when he said most of us would rather be dead than sensible.

ESMÉ   How right he was. The human capacity for mental inertia is limitless.

NOËL   *You* redressed the balance a bit, anyway. (*nostalgically*) *Charley's*

Aunt! I wonder what happened to them all. Dead as mutton, I suppose.

ESMÉ   Not necessarily. I'm sure I saw Enid Groome's name in something the other day, and Aubrey Carruthers was only about five years older than us. *Such* a good-looking boy.

NOËL   Aubrey! How one forgets.

ESMÉ   Little Audrey as we called him — because we weren't quite sure.

NOËL   Oh, *I* was sure. There was a distinct rapport.

ESMÉ   (*with coolness*) He was charming to *everyone*, quite indiscriminately. With me there *was* a tendresse. I remember walking with him on the Devil's Dyke when we were playing Brighton. He told me about his perfectly appalling childhood and dragon of a mother, and how he had suffered at school. He said, ''Darling, you must learn to accept that the world is antagonistic to those of special susceptibilities. We shall always feel alone.'' He was *so* sensitive.

NOËL   That was word for word what he said to *me* in a tea shop in Chipping Sodbury when we were playing Bristol.

Esmé rises, and as the scene continues begins to improve the flower arrangements and place the still-wrapped displays in more attractive groupings.

ESMÉ   (*casually*) Well, of course, it doesn't matter in the very least, darling, but I do assure you that he was in fact devoted to *me*.

NOËL   Well, darling, you go on thinking that if it comforts you. In point of fact, for all his good looks, he was as feeble as a cup of China tea and has never been heard of since.

ESMÉ   He had private means, poor lamb. The ruin of a weak man. I imagine some predatory creature got her teeth into him eventually.

NOËL   Some predatory creature usually does. Or, like you, they marry some horny male who naturally continues to rush around proving his virility with all and sundry. And they say women are instinctive! My God, it's hotter than ever in here!

ESMÉ   They *are* instinctive, but not always about the right qualities.

In Lynden's case, if only he had remained faithful to Christian Science, he would never have looked sideways. *That* was his undoing.

NOËL   I thought it was that busty Mrs Oliver who was his undoing.

ESMÉ   She was the catalyst. The real problem was spiritual.

NOËL   Well, well!

ESMÉ   Do you remember, soon after I married, when Lynden took me to see *The Passing of the Third Floor Back* in Chelsea, and I burst into tears on the bus going back to Battersea because I had thought it was going to help me to understand?

NOËL   (*affectionately*) Of course I do, my darling old cow. You have always felt everything much much too much.

ESMÉ   You poor pet, what I put you through when I was in agonies over Val. Not that you didn't get your own back after you had met that friend of Johnny Ekins . . .

NOËL   (*rising*) Oh, God, how painful it can be looking back!

He makes for cigarette box, remembers, swerves toward drink cupboard, gestures despairingly, then returns to chair.

Sorry! The old leg twinges from time to time. I suppose you don't have a Polo mint about you?

ESMÉ   (*sitting on arm of* NOËL's *chair*) Poor darling! (*strokes his hair above one ear*) This *beastly* business of seeming to get old.

NOËL   "Seeming" is a massive understatement.

ESMÉ   Time is only another form of error, darling.

NOËL   To think we could once count the future in decades. I view this ageing process with profound disapproval.

ESMÉ   It is not the real you. Just cling to that.

NOËL   The unreal me is still passionately attached to eating, drinking and moderate copulation, and it doesn't want to die.

ESMÉ   You must focus on the reality, not the illusion.

NOËL   Precisely what I was trying to do only seconds before you came on the 'phone.

Door bell rings.

Come!

WAITER *enters.*

The temperature is ten degrees higher since you kicked tha
thing.

WAITER   (*shrugging*) Some go one way, some the other. He'll be alon
              soon. (*puts glass on table*)

              ESMÉ *smiles at waiter who exits with a glance at the ceiling and th
              expression of one who has seen it all.*

ESMÉ   Dear Mrs Eddy said once . . .
NOËL   Stoj, duckie, you know what I think about Mrs Eddy, so don'
              let's ruin a beautiful reunion by dragging her on stage. A shad
              further down behind the ear would be heavenly. No one ha
              tickled the soles of my feet like you used to.
ESMÉ   But darling, one can't just extinguish a huge fund of gratitude
              I owe so much to Christian Science.
NOËL   (*raising a hand*) Remember our palship pact? That we'd neve
              again argue about religion? It probably saved one, if not both
              of our lives.
ESMÉ   What else is worthy of argument?
NOËL   Don't let's argue at all. Let's just remember.
ESMÉ   At our seeming age we should be looking to the future, no
              the past.
NOËL   You see? You're as bad as I am.
ESMÉ   Not as bad. Just more organized for the next stage.
NOËL   But the past has been fun, and the present — give or take a
              virus or two — has looked distinctly rosier ever since Joe Glaze
              offered me an absurd sum to come out here and warble at the
              natives. The future is utterly unpredictable and may come to
              a grinding halt at any moment.
ESMÉ   All the more reason for seeing the priorities. Before it's too late
NOËL   Too late for what? (*rising*) Perhaps a tiny tonic water woul
              not be too demoralizing. (*he pours this and furtively adds som
              gin before returning to chair*)
ESMÉ   Don't you see that it's just because our limited human minds
              can't foresee the future that we should prepare ourselves to
              cope with it?

NOËL	That sounds very Irish. If there is nothing ahead but a limitless morass of mindless gunge, I see no point in discussing it.
ESMÉ	What an uninspiring vision from a creative, imaginative man!
NOËL	Well, I'll bet you half a crown that the jolly old future is not just one vast meadow with Binkie Beaumont, Norah Howard and Gertie knee-deep in buttercups and daisies. You may return to my ear. (ESMÉ *does so*)
ESMÉ	Maybe it is whatever we want to find at the end of the rainbow.
NOËL	That's more my girl! Do you remember that first year?
ESMÉ	Of *Where the Rainbow Ends*? Of course.
NOËL	Mary Martin, Gertie Millar, Lily Elsie — none of them has held half the glamour you had for me as Rosamund. First impressions . . .
ESMÉ	I was thinking only the other day of darling Hawtrey.
NOËL	Darling Hawtrey! How I tormented him.
ESMÉ	You were *so* cheeky. So persistent.
NOËL	(*sighing*) Nineteen thirteen.
ESMÉ	(*sharply*) Nineteen eleven.
NOËL	Thirteen.
ESMÉ	Eleven. Have you forgotten that sheaf of corrections I had to send you when *Present Indicative* was published?
NOËL	I papered the Gerald Road loo with them, darling.
ESMÉ	You're hopeless with dates. Hawtrey gave me the lead in the *Rainbow* in 1911.
NOËL	God, I was jealous! Well, not jealous, perhaps . . .
ESMÉ	(*firmly*) Jealous. And it was during that first run — remember? — that he put on the fairy play I wrote for a special children's matinée at the Savoy. He did adore me so, bless him!
NOËL	Could I ever forget? It implanted my overwhelming desire to be a writer.
ESMÉ	Yes, but I think that was your natural competitiveness as much as jealousy.
NOËL	Certainly. ''Jealousy'' would imply I didn't think I could write too.
ESMÉ	(*drily*) It took some time.
NOËL	Well, it wasn't for lack of being egged on by you. I'll concede that.

ESMÉ   I could tell the spark was there.

NOËL   Anyway, to know a leading lady and playwright rolled into
           one podgy little girl was heady stuff in 1913.

ESMÉ   Eleven. And I was never podgy. A little intense at times, which
           is why you called me "Stodge", but never podgy. *You* were.
           Which is why I called you "Podge".

NOËL   Darling old Stojkins, I don't know why I didn't call you
           "Trout". You rise every time.

ESMÉ   That button's loose.

NOËL   Gary has just sewn it back on.

ESMÉ   *And* you've managed to tear your dressing gown. Give me
           a needle.

NOËL   I don't know where it's kept. I do hope Coley hurries up and
           convinces his virus it is only error.

'Phone rings. NOËL *answers it.*

Seven O three. (*puts hand over mouthpiece*) It's a female
headhunter from Memphis who's moved in on Vegas recently
and is a perfect plague. She wasn't invited to my party the
other night and she's obviously livid. (*into 'phone*) My dear,
dear Mrs Logan, you are kindness itself, but there isn't the
smallest inch of space left in my schedule before I head back
for London. (*to* ESMÉ) Her single-mindedness would have
humbled even Mrs Eddy. (*into 'phone*) No, Mrs Logan; please,
Mrs Logan, you simply must accept my state of hideous over-
commitment. I am desolate I cannot take up your invitation,
but such disappointments are the tragic penalty of a certain
notoriety. Besides, I have been struck down by a virus that
makes any kind of intercourse quite unthinkable . . . I regret.
I really do regret . . . (*puts down receiver despite audible resistance.*
ESMÉ *returns to his ear*)

ESMÉ   You don't imagine *that's* going to put her off?

NOËL   I can't be too rude. *Mr* Logan is buying up Vegas rapidly and
           has money in my show. When the organ grinds, the monkey
           must earn his nuts.

ESMÉ   What does she want? Your party's over now, so it can't be that.

NOËL   I think she's set up some sort of salon in Vegas . . .

ESMÉ   Don't you mean "saloon"?

NOËL   Unfortunately, no. I believe she fancies herself as the hostess
with the mostest, and I've a nasty feeling she intends to crash
a small farewell do I had planned in the Sky Room. Her aims
are not entirely clear, but my instincts tell me she is up to no
good.

ESMÉ   It's probably you she's after.

NOËL   Only a natural modesty prevented it crossing my mind.

ESMÉ   They can be so forceful, these Americans. Such a strong
presence. When Orson prepares my audience with his
introduction, I feel they want to give me serious attention.

NOËL   Americans give everything serious attention. It's rather sweet.

ESMÉ   It is also exhausting. I quite firmly agreed with the people in
London to no more than ten lectures with two days' rest
between each. I've already done fifteen, and if Orson had had
his way today I would have been flown home on a stretcher.
He needs some man to speak to him firmly. Could you be an
angel?

NOËL   (*his eyes half closed*) Shift your attention to the other ear, and
I shall be in a mood to consider almost anything.

ESMÉ   I know Orson admires you tremendously. But I'm hopeless
about business matters, and he knows it. If you were to tell
him that if he tries to push me beyond the terms of my contract, I shan't be able to give of my best, I am sure he would
respect your professional judgment.

NOËL   My professional judgment is that you are as strong as a horse
and could cope nightly plus matinées, just as *I* do on drink,
cigarettes, red meat, and incessant sex, but I'll certainly 'phone
him.

ESMÉ   Bless you! This is his number. (*she hands him card;* NOËL
pockets it)

Door bell rings.

NOËL   Thank heaven! The air conditioning man. (*going to door*) I'm
so vulnerable without Coley. (*he opens door. More flowers can
be seen*) Oh, no! Where is that damned engineer?

BELLBOY *enters with flowers.*

I'm going to be a month of Sundays writing thank-you letters. (*he points to bedroom on right*) Put them in there. No, hang
on! Stoj, duckie, what's your room number?

ESMÉ   Ten thousand . . . no, *one* thousand and three.

NOËL   (*to* BELLBOY) Take them to room number one thousand and
three.

ESMÉ   How sweet of you, darling.

NOËL   An act of pure self-preservation. I'd better just see who they're
from. (*looks at card*) Darling Lornie. How suitable. She'd love
you to have them.

BELLBOY *exits with flowers after receiving tip.*

ESMÉ   It's like being back in the theatre.

NOËL   (*flinging himself into chair*) Golly, the work we got through in
those days!

ESMÉ   *More*, perhaps, but it was less demanding. You wouldn't
believe how much research has gone into the books I write
now.

NOËL   You shouldn't have become such a highbrow.

ESMÉ   We must follow our star.

NOËL   If your father had had his way, I suppose you'd have gone
to Girton and worn blue stockings and a bun instead of
frittering your early days with me.

ESMÉ   You were much more fun than Girton. Anyway, Mummy and
I were both determined I should go on the stage, so Daddy
didn't have a chance.

NOËL   Not that your mama lacked reservations about my influence
on you.

ESMÉ   (*laughs*) Remember the first line you wrote for me in *I'll Leave
It To You*? (*quotes*) ''Oh, mother, isn't he cynical?''

NOËL   Your *first* line was a rather inane giggle.

ESMÉ   A giggle isn't a line. At the most, it's an interjection.

NOËL   (*sighing*) You were always so exact. Oh, if only, if only . . .

ESMÉ   If only what?

NOËL   If only we could have gone on from there. From you being Faith in that play, and I being Bobbie. (*quoting*) ''Oh, Faith, we'll have the most wonderful times in the world — just you and me together; say you're happy, say you're excited about it.''

ESMÉ   (*slipping back into the part*) ''I'm absolutely thrilled — I'm . . .''

NOËL   And then your mother — well, Mrs Crombie — came in.

ESMÉ   I should get a royalty for all the autobiographical bits you've put in your plays.

NOËL   Isn't it extraordinary how easily one can slip back? (*he gets up and begins to act a part; quoting*) ''I've had a perfectly miserable night. I couldn't sleep a wink. I want to know if you really meant what you said last night.''

ESMÉ *stands and moves about.*

ESMÉ   ''Of course I really meant it. How silly you are.''

GARY *enters in a hurry.*

GARY   Can you believe? Made it to the bus stop before I missed my money. (*seeing* ESMÉ) Oh, pardon me!

NOËL   (*gesturing, but not speaking to him*) ''I'm not silly. I thought maybe it was only the heat of the moment that made you so utterly beastly.''

ESMÉ   ''If you're going to be rude I shall go away.'' (*sits in chair*)

NOËL   (*with extra stress*) ''Do you really care for me so little that you can give me up at a moment's notice like that?''

GARY *is no longer hurrying. He has very slowly made his way round the room and finds his money on a chair, but his attention is elsewhere.*

ESMÉ   ''You will not understand, Bobbie. I had to.''

NOËL   ''Why?''

ESMÉ   ''Because Mother made me promise.''

GARY's *jaw drops a little.* NOËL *goes to piano. As scene proceeds he picks out notes and sings lines from the song ''Faith'' from* I'll Leave it to You

NOËL	"*What* did she make you promise?"
ESMÉ	"She made me promise that . . . that . . ."
NOËL	"Well?"
ESMÉ	"Well, you see, I'm an only child, and Mother wants me to be happy above all things, and . . ."
NOËL	"I could make you happy — wonderfully happy."
GARY	Jeez!
ESMÉ	"Mother doesn't think so. You see I've always been used to having money and comforts and things."
NOËL	"Do you imagine that I shouldn't have been able to give you all the comforts you wanted whether I had uncle's money or not? Why, in a year or so I shall be making hundreds. I mean to be successful — nothing will stop me."
GARY	You gotta be play-acting.
NOËL	(*irritably*) Well of course we are play-acting, you ass. Do stop interrupting. I thought you were in a rush to get somewhere.
GARY	Yeah, well, I was . . . am . . . (*goes to door*) Well, pardon (*to* ESMÉ), miss . . . ma'am . . . (*exits in confusion*)
NOËL	A nice lad but as thick as two boards and with a memory like a sieve. (*he leaves piano*)
ESMÉ	It seems we can still hold an audience.
NOËL	(*half wistful, half tetchy*) What an absolute chump you were to give it all up.
ESMÉ	Darling, don't let's go through that again. And anyway, what I gave up was nothing to what I put in its place.
NOËL	But you could have been a household name.
ESMÉ	I didn't *want* to be a household name. Lifebuoy Soap is a household name. I wanted to find the Truth, and having found it, to give it to others.
NOËL	(*sits*) The truth, darling, was that you gave up a brilliant career to write exceedingly dull books that no one in their right senses could want to read.
ESMÉ	That is deliberately provocative and totally untrue.
NOËL	It is as true as the chins on my face, and just as tragic. You and I could have achieved so much together.

ESMÉ *returns to rearranging flowers and generally tidying.*

ESMÉ   I had to choose between going into one trivial play after another, and writing what could really help people to see an alternative to this awful jungle of human life.

NOËL   My dear old Guernsey, you can't say those rather fruity novels Collins published *helped* anyone.

ESMÉ   They were stepping stones. I doubt if you've read *one* of my later books, even though I sent them to you.

NOËL   I tried manfully to come to terms with them and decided you should have stuck to the stage.

ESMÉ   At the level of *I'll Leave It To You*?

NOËL   I wrote you that far longer part in *The Young Idea*, and what did you do? Renounce the stage!

ESMÉ   The wife of Lynden's commanding officer in Scotland was responsible for that. She said I wouldn't make a success of my marriage if I did stage work in London, with my husband hundreds of miles away.

NOËL   And much good *that* advice did you! Your marriage was a total disaster. If you had stayed with me I'd have written parts for you until the cows came home and Gertie would never have had to take your place.

ESMÉ   No one could have taken my place, least of all Gertie. And anyway, I never grudged what you did for her.

NOËL   That's not the point. If ever jolly old destiny or the Truth or divine Mind or whatever had set two people up for the partnership of a lifetime, it was in 1913.

ESMÉ   Eleven.

NOËL   Whereupon you promptly ruined everything by embracing marriage and that dratted Christian Science with an enthusiasm only equalled by wishful thinking and sheer wilful obstinacy. Must you fiddle with those flowers? You're so restless.

ESMÉ   You really should put them into water. At least I wanted to grow. To develop.

NOËL   And I haven't, I suppose.

ESMÉ   Not very much, no.

NOËL   I doubt if you've even *seen* my later plays.

ESMÉ   Yes I have. You gave me seats for *Blithe Spirit*. You only wrote it to annoy me.

NOËL   You laughed like a drain.

ESMÉ   A sense of humour has nothing to do with a deeply held faith.

NOËL   Then it bloody well ought to have. Anyway, I have written rather more than *Blithe Spirit* since the 1920s.

ESMÉ   I don't have time to go to the theatre.

NOËL   You have time to whizz round the United States of America giving spiritual jabs to blue-rinsed matrons with doubts about their hereafters.

ESMÉ   You of all people should know it is vital to stick to one's guns.

NOËL   What a metaphor for a pacifist!

ESMÉ   Much of your antagonism toward all I stand for is rooted in the fear of admitting to what you know would invalidate your whole life.

NOËL   God, how patronizing you can be! (*he lights a cigarette and inhales greedily*) And if this is bloody error, then whoopee! (*the last word is spoken huskily*) There you are! See what you've done! My voice is conking out again.

ESMÉ   It has managed pretty well so far.

NOËL   Thank you for that ready sympathy.

Door bell rings. NOËL *opens it.*

ENG.   Got a bit of trouble?

NOËL   Much, much more than a bit.

ENGINEER *enters and goes to air conditioning unit below window.*

(*to* ESMÉ) Believe it or not, my voice is rather important to me.

The ENGINEER, *seemingly oblivious to all else, attacks the unit with a variety of tools and appliances, and from a number of prone and upright positions, whistling tunelessly through his teeth.*

ESMÉ   It is a pity you don't put it to better use than jeering at everything I stand for.

NOËL   (*coughing, clearing his throat, and rubbing it*) This is disastrous. I shall probably not be able to perform again for a week.

ESMÉ   If you paid as much attention to your spiritual condition as to your physical, such symptoms of error wouldn't affect you.

NOËL   (*glaring at her and feeling his throat tenderly*) Really, Stoj! I do not know why — long, long ago — some public-spirited citizen did not halve you from top to toe with a meat-axe. But I suppose if they had, Mrs Eddy would have seen to it that there were two of you. A sort of spiritual earthworm.

ESMÉ   Not everyone is as terrified as you are of the Truth.

NOËL   I haven't done all that badly with error.

ESMÉ   Exactly. You have committed the worst of crimes. You have refused to evolve. Instead of realizing your spiritual potentialities, you have perfected imperfection for the sake of money and a rather shallow fame.

NOËL   You, on the other hand, have so imperfectly cultivated perfection that you are having to scuttle round America at the beck of your publisher for fear that he ditches your contract.

ESMÉ   When I realized how much they needed a better sense of direction over here, I saw that my tour was probably meant.

NOËL   I'd forgotten ''meant''! So convenient! Coley won't be able to find a thing, if you don't leave this place alone.

ESMÉ   Poj, darling, it's no good your getting petulant. I have known you longer than anyone living, bar your mother, and probably *better* than she did because mother love is so blinding. We were more inseparable than most brothers and sisters and I can trace your development with inch by inch accuracy.

NOËL   (*he rises and paces*) I did not develop inch by inch. I developed by leaps and bounds.

ESMÉ   In your career, yes. Spiritually you became a block of salt in your teens.

NOËL   Hawtrey and Gilbert Miller weren't buying my spirituality.

ESMÉ   But, darling, you *knew* so much more than you gave. Don't you remember how we both felt about that wicked first world war? All the young men we knew who would take us to the Carlton one moment and be blown sky-high the next.

NOËL   Of course I remember. We both lost boys who meant the world to us.

ESMÉ   The sheer unintelligence of the whole thing. And you reacted then. We used to sit our young men down and tell them to refuse to return to the Front. Why we weren't clapped into gaol for sedition, I shall never know.

NOËL   Well, at least you can't accuse me of going to the Front and adding to the carnage.

ESMÉ   No, but instead of having the moral courage to conscientiously object, which might have meant going to prison and no longer furthering your career, you wangled out of national service by drinking tea leaves and staging those tremendous nervous breakdowns.

NOËL   What earthly use was I to the Artists' Rifles? I could contribute much more by learning to entertain people. Anyway, you're forgetting *Post-Mortem*. A bitterly anti-war play.

ESMÉ   I don't forget it at all. The best thing you ever wrote so far as content was concerned. And what did you do with it? Hastily pushed it into your bottom drawer and wrote *Cavalcade* with your tongue in your cheek. I still have the copy you inscribed "With love from a National Hero."

NOËL   *Cavalcade* gave a huge number of people an immense amount of pleasure.

ESMÉ   So did the Empress Josephine.

NOËL   I have long suspected you hate my success.

ESMÉ   I don't hate it at all. What I hate is your willingness to be a spiritual trollop at the drop of a hat.

NOËL   In a moment I shall be pouring myself a stiff, stiff whisky.

ESMÉ   And then you will say even sillier things — if your voice survives smoke *and* alcohol. You never smoked or drank in the old days, any more than I did.

NOËL   Most of us grow up.

ESMÉ   We both thought it was darned unintelligent. We were rooted and grounded in Bernard Shaw, who so rightly said that the majority are always wrong.

NOËL   Sometimes one finds oneself among people who goad one into a state of merciful oblivion.

ESMÉ   If you drug your faculties, character suffers. When we were young, you were immense fun, utterly natural, had all your wits about you, were never snobbish . . .

NOËL   I am not in the least snobbish. I go out of my way to mix with other ranks.

ESMÉ   The second volume of your autobiography was almost devoid of humour . . .

NOËL   That's probably because you ticked me off about practically every line of the first. Sitting day after day on the john, looking at your reams of objections to *Present Indicative*, was deeply unsettling.

ESMÉ   As for that dreadful little book *Australia Revisited*, it was so full of pompous name-dropping — all those titles and ranks relentlessly spelled out in the footnotes — that I didn't know whether to roar with laughter or blush with shame.

NOËL   I'm sure you did both, incontinently. *Science and Health* affects me very similarly.

ESMÉ   I suppose the truth is that years of self-indulgence had blunted your judgment.

NOËL   Sometimes one has to play to the gallery.

ESMÉ   The audience for that snobbery-jobbery was not in the gallery, it was in the first eight rows of the stalls. You have social-climbed with merciless persistence ever since we went our separate ways.

NOËL   It is rather difficult *not* to get to know people when one is regarded as of star quality. Having chosen to live like a misanthropic hermit, you may not have grasped that simple truth.

ESMÉ   I am in constant touch with people of great distinction, but only if they can help to further my work. That is rather different from cultivating others for . . . well, more trivial reasons.

NOËL   Such as?

ESMÉ   You vowed you would get to the top, and in the career sense I always supported you to the hilt. But that wasn't enough for you. Your conquests had to be at every level . . .

NOËL   I'll bet we're getting on to sex now. I'm surprised it hasn't raised its ugly head before this.

ESMÉ   I'm not blaming you entirely for failing to outgrow that particular human weakness, because God alone knows how overpowering it can be, but to use it as a kind of social bait as though you were fly-fishing in Debrett, was disgusting.

NOËL   I don't know what you are talking about.

ESMÉ   You know perfectly well what I am talking about. You have always suffered at convenient moments from selective amnesia. A moment's weakness with a pretty chorus-boy is one thing; to make a dead set at royalty in a mere spirit of conquest — just to prove you could do it — was not the act of a grown man.

NOËL   I don't see what the bloody hell it has to do with you, Stoj, whether I have an affair with a prole or a prince.

ESMÉ   Then you shouldn't have succumbed to the temptation to brag about it.

NOËL   (*angrily*) This is utterly despicable of you. My friendship with you has been the most intimate I have had with any woman on earth. I've told you things no one else has known. To throw them back in my face as though you had a total monopoly on all virtue is . . . is . . . well, my God, words fail me.

He goes to drinks cupboard, removes decanter, bangs it down, takes out glass, opens bottle, shaking with rage.

ESMÉ   (*calmly, seeing to her face*) The worst aspect was that you knew them both and even spoke with seeming affection about the wife — the poor wretched woman.

NOËL   (*pouring a huge whisky*) What the bloody hell do you mean by "seeming affection"? I suppose it is beyond your grubby little imagination to understand that I was devoted to them equally.

ESMÉ   I shall give you enough credit not to take *that* too seriously.

NOËL   You know full well what I mean. She's a dear and we are still the greatest friends. I adore her.

ESMÉ   You chose a strange way of showing it.

NOËL   It was years ago, anyway. When we are young we do a lot of things we later regret.

ESMÉ   I don't believe you have regretted it for a minute until now.

NOËL   (*downing his drink*) My God, I shall have another. (*he pours*) And what have *you* regretted, may I ask, in your wasted, boring life of pummelling others' souls into submission?

ESMÉ   Nearly everything, as you should well know. It was a profound regret that compelled me to find a better pattern.

NOËL   And this is it! Being utterly odious to your oldest friend.

ESMÉ   You are so dedicated to pursuit of the transient that you have no inkling of what it means to have a true sense of mission.

NOËL   Missionaries end up in pots — with any luck.

He passes the teddy bear and thrusts the bottle angrily at its stomach. It topples to the floor.

ESMÉ   Darling, every word you utter is evidence of your spiritual immobility. It is ridiculous that a man of your intelligence, on the verge of old age, should have progressed not one inch beyond being a bright young thing of the 1920s.

NOËL   If spiritual maturity means being a pompous, preaching, out-of-touch travesty of Jesus Christ, then thank God for my eternal youth. (*waves bottle*) Have a double Scotch, you silly cow. Prove you're human.

ESMÉ   (*without a lot of compassion*) My poor Poj!

NOËL   God, you were such fun once upon a time. How tragically people can change.

ESMÉ   And how tragically they can stay the same.

NOËL   No one would believe you were the same person who was chased all down Clapham High Street when we stole those silk stockings.

ESMÉ   (*rattled*) That is totally untrue. It was you and Johnny Ekins who stole. I was an innocent bystander and terrified for both of you.

NOËL   Terrified or not, the stockings and the scent were awfully useful.

ESMÉ   (*with cold anger*) In the first place, Poj, the incident you mention was not in Clapham High Street, but the City, where Mummy and I had gone to meet Daddy. Secondly, it was not silk stockings or scent, it was books. I can remember to this day that awful chase by the bookseller, with Mummy and I looking on in horror. She nearly had a fit. I was convinced it was the end of your career and that you'd both be clapped into prison.

NOËL   (*beginning to enjoy himself again*) It's more blessed to give than to receive. You received the stockings and the scent with the alacrity of a starved ferret.

ESMÉ   Only that first time, before I knew what you had been doing.
            The way you made me out in your book to be a kind of fence
            for things I didn't dare steal myself was utterly unforgivable.

NOËL   Are you pretending that your childhood was one long summer
            of applied ethics?

ESMÉ   Of course not. Until I found Christian Science I wasn't ethical,
            but I was terribly cautious. I was desperately afraid of the law.
            There's no *virtue* in that; it just happens to be a fact. You, on
            the other hand, had no fear of anything. You doubtless relied
            on saying something funny and making the policeman laugh.
            You were so assured. It was because I was terrified that you
            and Johnny were going to ruin your lives that I said I wouldn't
            dream of accepting the things you stole. I always remember
            darling John saying, "Well, we owe it to Stoj that we're not
            both in prison."

            GARY *enters, again in a hurry. He is ignored.*

GARY   One foot on the bus and I remembered I'd forgotten my script.
            (*takes playscript from mantelpiece*)

NOËL   (*to* ESMÉ) It is quite marvellous the way every highpoint of
            your life resounds to your credit.

ESMÉ   I wish I could say the same of you. The tragic thing about your
            life is not that it has been shallow and unregenerate, but that
            you suffer no spark of remorse.

NOËL   (*furious*) Now listen to me once for all, you bloody infuriating
            woman — I don't happen to believe that I have any good
            reason to suffer remorse. In my fashion, by my own lights,
            I have lived by a certain moral code and have nothing — well,
            very little — to reproach myself for.

            GARY *is now perched on the drinks cupboard, smiling and gesturing
            knowingly, as one enjoying a familiar show.*

ESMÉ   Then you should add shame to remorse. Not only have you
            failed lamentably to live up to the best you knew, but you have

sought consistently to pull down to your own level, by gross misrepresentation of their actions and motives, those who have tried to live by a higher code.

NOËL   (*spluttering*) Hah! ''Those who have tried to live by a higher code'' being you, of course.

GARY   (*nodding vigorously with approval*) Hey, this is great play-acting! When does it hit Broadway?

NOËL   (*turning on him*) What the bloody hell have you come back for? You're like a Jack-in-the-box. Bugger off!

GARY   (*startled, moving quickly*) O.K.! Sorry! Didn't mean to intrude! (*he falls over the teddy bear and puts it back against the wall*) Sorry! (*exits*)

ESMÉ   At least I have held fast to my faith in the Highest Good and have helped others to share in it.

NOËL   By nagging and criticizing and writing unreadable religious tracts.

ESMÉ   Books, not tracts, and they are certainly not unreadable. Even darling Ivor had one by his bed the day he died.

NOËL   I hesitate to trace the possible connection.

ESMÉ   Just because he wrote romantic plays and wasn't as quick and nasty as you, you have always been snide about Ivor.

NOËL   Rubbish! I adored Ivor.

ESMÉ   Most people ''adore'' steak. It doesn't do the bull much good.

NOËL   Now don't you start on that.

ESMÉ   I am not starting on anything. I am just pointing out that dear Ivor was perfectly capable of reading my books. But then he was such a different cup of tea from you. Warm, loving, sweet, and interested in the path I had taken since leaving the stage. Not childishly jeering and insensitive.

NOËL   Well, I'm sorry, duckie, but I think I am of moderate intelligence, and I found your recent tomes about as snappy as a Russian translation of Sir Walter Scott.

ESMÉ   Most people don't dip into the Bible and William Shakespeare in the expectation of finding them snappy.

NOËL   Well at least they strike a *few* chords in the common breast.

ESMÉ   But you won't bother with *anything* I produce! What about the novels I wrote with darling J.D.? Even *you* could have understood those if you had tried.

NOËL   Oh, yes, I had forgotten poor old Beresford. Well, I did read
         one of your collaborations, and I can tell you here and now
         it wasn't a patch on *The Hampdenshire Wonder* and the other
         stuff he wrote before you came along and snapped him up.

ESMÉ   I don't know what you mean by "snapped him up."

NOËL   His wife knew.

ESMÉ   Really, Noël, is there no limit to your libellous perversion of
         the truth?

NOËL   The truth was that you plunged into a rip-roaring late affair
         with a man old enough to be your father.

ESMÉ   (*furious*) You know perfectly well that my relationship with
         J.D. was purely mental.

NOËL   (*provocatively*) A likely story!

ESMÉ   Likely or not in the degenerate and cynical world you choose
         to inhabit, it happens to be absolutely true.

NOËL   How long did you live together? Ten years?

ESMÉ   We *collaborated* for *eight*. And as you are fully aware, we lived
         in guest houses, in separate rooms, except for the two years
         near Oxford when I made sure Jon was in by ten every even-
         ing to chaperone us.

NOËL   And what, pray, was likely to happen at ten that couldn't have
         happened at eight-thirty?

ESMÉ   It was necessary for the relationship not only to *be* right, but
         to be *seen* to be right.

NOËL   Well, I know I am shallow and superficial and a spiritual disaster
         area, but from what you have told me in the past of his wife's
         reactions I am afraid I am another sceptic just like her.

ESMÉ   You know very well that J.D. was near the end of his life, had
         nothing in common with Trissie any more, and felt he had
         written himself out. With my help he was able to produce
         several more novels which incidentally were very well
         received.

NOËL   Rave notices in Psychic News, no doubt.

ESMÉ   Leading national reviews. Why must you belittle everything?

NOËL   I've learned from my spiritual betters.

ESMÉ   I wish you had. J.D. had one of the most open, enquiring and
         humane minds of his generation.

NOËL	A pity his generation didn't acknowledge it more handsomely.
ESMÉ	That is a reflection on the generation, not on J.D.
NOËL	Just as well you went on extracting an allowance from Lynden.
ESMÉ	(*upset, but holding back tears*) I can't understand your cruelty, Poj. Do you really grudge me so bitterly the few years J.D. and I spent together? Do you think it has been easy for me to adjust to being alone since he passed on?
NOËL	You've had Jon.
ESMÉ	Who has been foolish enough to marry a hopelessly unsuitable girl and is struggling against heavy odds to make enough money to pay for his mistakes.
NOËL	No one forced you to cut yourself off from life. If we choose our beds, we must lie on them.
ESMÉ	We don't choose our priorities, and the stars we follow, the way we choose a washing powder.
NOËL	Spare me the metaphysical truisms.
ESMÉ	That's the trouble. You have been spared metaphysical truisms all your life, as your values and outlook amply prove.
NOËL	Really, Stoj, your unutterable gall is almost worthy of admiration. You stand there like St Peter at the pearly gates, banishing me to the nether regions with a long list of my crimes, yet every single instance of your own givings-in to ''error'' has to be presented as a blameless addition to your unremitting efforts to contribute to the Highest Good.
ESMÉ	By their works they shall be known.
NOËL	Look, I'm not blaming you for grabbing another woman's husband in your ripe middle years, any more than I blamed you for bouncing around having affairs left, right and centre before you were decently into your teens . . .
ESMÉ	Now what nonsense are you adding to your muck-raking?
NOËL	Val, Teddy, that Lord Whatshisname, Hawtrey — are you pretending . . . ?
ESMÉ	I could hardly be blamed for young men being infatuated. That didn't mean to say . . .
NOËL	Hawtrey wasn't exactly a callow youth . . .
ESMÉ	I am glad you are not suggesting I tried to corrupt him.
ENG.	O.K., you're fixed.

NOËL   (*to* ESMÉ) It is you who equates sex with corruption. (*to* ENGINEER) My dear fellow! Marvellous.

ENGINEER *goes to door. He turns and gives* NOËL *a sympathetic wink.*

ENG.   Yeah, man, I reckon you are fixed — but good! (*exits*)

NOËL   No, I suppose once more you would have me believe that in every thought and act you have been motivated throughout your life by a God-given sense of the good and the true and the pure.

ESMÉ   (*near to tears*) I have tried, yes. *Really* tried. Why can't you understand that it was because I had fallen so short of the ideal when I was young, that I have done my best to make amends since? If only you had once known what it is like to feel real shame, you would see me in a different light.

NOËL   It defeats me why, if you have such a low opinion of me, you should bother to seek me out in Vegas when you could be devoting every minute to placing the feet of the unregenerate natives on the shining path to spiritual evolution.

ESMÉ   In a place as soulless as Las Vegas, any human contact from the past seemed comforting.

NOËL   Thank you very much! Charming!

ESMÉ   Oh, look at the time! (*rising*) My car should be waiting. May I use the bathroom?

NOËL   Of course. The loo has been sanitized. I've not touched the towels on the shelf. The chance of your contracting syphilis is practically nil.

ESMÉ *enters bedroom up left.*

(*calling*) Drape a towel over the bidet if it offends.

He pours another drink and sips it. He pauses, the glass at his mouth, then lowers it, obviously struck by an idea. He smiles, goes to bedroom door and gently closes it, then takes card from his pocket and goes to the 'phone. He lights a cigarette, then dials.

I would like to speak to Mr Orson Humdinger . . . It is? My
name is Noël Coward . . . You do? How flattering . . . You're
too kind . . . Yes, they do seem to like it. Now forgive me,
Mr Humdinger . . . May I really? Well, Orson, then — forgive
me for bothering you, but I have Esmé Wynne-Tyson with
me . . . Yes, isn't she? Such a chirpy little thing. (*he makes a
face at the bedroom door*) Packed with *joie de vivre*. Now, look,
I believe your car is taking her to a meeting shortly . . . Fine!
Well, she's had a little rest, so I'm sure she will be raring to
go. Orson, I am ringing you because Esmé is quite upset that
she refused your marvellous offer to get her a spot in the
Tabitha Tabernacle service this evening. She feels you must
think her terribly ungrateful . . . How generous of you to take
that view . . . Now, we are old friends, as you may know.
I've given her a little talking to — I am one of the few people
she will listen to, you know — and she is now utterly convinced it is a splendid idea. She was a wonderful little actress
in her early years, you know. Before she found the Truth and
all that kind of thing. In the course of our chat I managed to
persuade her of the tremendous possibilities in appearing at
the Tabernacle, and I have suggested that if you are agreeable
she should make a surprise entrance with all the fixings, and
with you of course waiting on the stage to greet and introduce
her . . . But perhaps it is too late now? And then there are
the Quakers . . . You really think you can? . . . Marvellous!
. . . Trumpets? Yes, I'm sure she'd adore trumpets . . .
Garlands? Well, why not? . . . A band? My dear Orson, that
would do nicely. And isn't there a Tabitha team of cheer-
leaders for special events? . . . Fabulous! You'll ring them at
once? Orson, what an organizer you must be. How I curse
this stupid virus for preventing me being there. But look here,
Orson, she wants this to be utterly secret until the very last
moment. Can you get your driver on the 'phone? . . . Splendid! Then make sure he doesn't mention where he's taking
her. Don't make contact with her until she is swept up to you
in the stadium. I have her keyed up like a finely tuned violin.
The least disturbance could send her off the whole idea. I know

her temperament so well, you see . . . Tremendous! Wonderful! How well you understand the soul of the artist . . . Bless you, yes, we must . . . She'll be on her way in just a moment . . . Goodbye! (ESMÉ *enters*) Just about to check that your car has arrived.

ESMÉ   Don't bother. I will wait in my room if necessary.

NOËL   (*replacing receiver*) As you wish. (*striking a tragic pose*) I suppose it is not of the slightest importance to you that I am deeply, deeply hurt?

ESMÉ   (*coldly*) If there is a spark of genuine feeling anywhere within you, you should be deeply, deeply ashamed. Don't trouble to see me out. (*she exits*)

NOËL *follows her to the archway. As the front door closes he embraces the teddy bear emotionally, leaning his head on its shoulder and slapping its back slowly with one hand, shaking with amusement.*

CURTAIN

ACT TWO

The next morning. GARY *is alone on stage. He marches several times from the drinks cupboard to centre stage with a bamboo cane on his shoulder. On each occasion he halts, comes to attention, slopes arms, then stands at ease. From the bedroom comes a low, rising moo that reaches a strained crescendo, before descending to an exhausted croak.* GARY's *eyes turn to the ceiling and he clicks his tongue. He repeats the drill. The mooing gets louder and more absurd.*

GARY   (*flinging cane on couch*) Oh, for Pete's sake!

NOËL   (*off*) Did you say something, dear boy?

GARY   Not so as you'd notice. I'm rehearsing.

NOËL *enters in dressing gown and trousers.*

NOËL   My God, it's like a refrigerator in here!

GARY   It's your unit.

NOËL   If anyone says that again, I shall probably brain them. (*he rubs his throat*) But thank heaven at least for Alf Dixon. I really believe he's chased off that nasty old error.

GARY   Sounded like you were giving a pint of cream. Guess I'd better get to the theatre.

NOËL   Of course you must. I'll survive somehow. Do you know your lines?

GARY   I've only got one.

NOËL   (*firmly*) One is a start.

GARY   (*picking up cane and rehearsing*) I walk out from behind a pillar and kind of come to attention with my spear. (*he stands at ease, the tip of the cane rather near* NOËL's *eye.* NOËL *backs away*) Then I say, "The king is without."

NOËL   Without what? The audience will be agog.

GARY   (*gloomily*) I'm capable of better things.

NOËL	We all are, Gary. Just ask Stoj. With the help of the divine Mind you could have Gielgud cringing and Olivier in helpless hysterics. Now do give me the full flavour — just once.

GARY, embarrassed, plays his scene — not very well.

GARY	(*standing at ease*) The king is without.
NOËL	Yes, I think I can speak for both John *and* Larry.
GARY	It's not a part I wouldn't sacrifice if something turned up in London.
NOËL	I quite understand that, dear boy. You won't be forgotten, I promise.
GARY	You mean . . . ?
NOËL	Send me your press notices. Every one. I shall file them with the greatest care. One never knows.
GARY	That's great! Thanks a lot!
NOËL	So there we are, Gary. Thank you for your devoted nannying.
GARY	You're not angry I've got full-time rehearsals?
NOËL	Of course not. Work must come first. I'm back to London tomorrow anyway, with or without Coley.
GARY	I've learned a lot being with you, Mr Coward.
NOËL	So have I, dear boy, so have I. Are you sure you won't stay to breakfast?
GARY	I'd better be going. This is goodbye, then.
NOËL	Only, I hope, *au revoir.*
GARY	I'll be thinking of you.
NOËL	(*with sincerity*) So shall I.
GARY	So long, then. Don't forget to gargle.
NOËL	*Arrivederci,* my dear Gary. (*they shake hands*) And do be careful with that spear.

GARY exits, picking up a grip by the door. NOËL *removes his dressing gown and begins his exercises. The 'phone rings and he answers it.*

(*imitating* GARY's *voice*) Mr Coward's suite . . . (*in his own voice*) And good morning to *you,* desk . . . (*looks at watch*) Well, I suppose you'd better . . . Yes, all right, put her on . . . Hullo,

Stoj! Did you sleep well . . . Sorry, it's only polite to ask . . .
Yes, I'm alone, but . . . (*he looks at receiver, grimaces, and replaces it. He puts on dressing gown, sees to his hair in mirror, unlocks door, then enters bedroom and is heard gargling*)

Door bell rings and WAITER *enters with breakfast trolley.*

(*off*) *That* was quick, darling. You must have whizzed up like a rocket.

WAITER *looks at ceiling and arranges trolley.*

WAITER	We try, Mr Coward. We try.
NOËL	(*entering*) Oh, my dear chap . . .
WAITER	Sunnyside up, wasn't it?
NOËL	(*cautiously*) What was?
WAITER	Your egg.
NOËL	Sunny if you will, but not runny.
WAITER	Firm but yielding, that's what chef goes for. Firm but yielding, like a woman's body. There was a guy in six thirty-four . . .
NOËL	Yes, well you must tell me all about it some time, but it's a little early and a friend is on her way up.
WAITER	(*with meaning*) Aha! O.K., Mr Coward, I'm in the picture. No problem. You just have a nice . . . breakfast.
NOËL	I shall try.
WAITER	Say, it's nice and cool in here.
NOËL	It is arctic.
WAITER	No problem. (*he kicks the unit twice, once on each end*) Never fails. (*exits*)

The unit makes a strange whining rattle, then falls silent. NOËL *looks at it distrustfully. The bell rings.* NOËL *crosses room and opens door.* ESMÉ *enters under full sail.*

NOËL	(*rather too gaily*) Darling! Just in time for breakfast.
ESMÉ	(*huskily*) Poj! How *could* you!
NOËL	In the state of gibbering fury you drove me to last night —

with the utmost ease. The whole scene cried out for a touch of comedy.

ESMÉ   It was unforgivable.

NOËL   *You* were unforgivable.

ESMÉ   For a grown man to descend to such a cruel practical joke . . .

NOËL   You have told me incessantly that I am not a grown man, so I have faced the Truth. I'm spiritually inadequate. A moral babe.

ESMÉ   You don't have to be spiritually adequate to know the rules of common decency.

NOËL   My dear old cow, when one is in a towering rage, deeply hurt, bitterly disillusioned, the last thing to float into the turmoil of one's bruised, bewildered mind is common decency. Now, come on, get some breakfast inside you. Gary's left, so you can have his cup. The spiritual you won't have a chance in hell unless it starts the day with a good breakfast.

ESMÉ   I can only thank God that my voice failed me.

NOËL   (*delighted*) It did? Well, you can thank my virus, not God.

ESMÉ   Nonsense! I merely suffered the most intense attack of stage fright I have ever known.

NOËL   Then why are you croaking like something in a swamp?

ESMÉ   I've told you. Sheer nerves. Even Orson realized I couldn't go on in that state.

NOËL   You're out of practice. Now sit down and have a hot toasted bun.

They sit, but ESMÉ *is not thinking about food.*

ESMÉ   What would *you* have done if you had been expecting a small group of elderly Quakers, then found yourself confronted by a vast ocean of black faces, all chanting and swooning and . . . well, never mind the details?

NOËL   I would have romped into a spirited rendering of ''Mad Dogs'', done a little dance, and had them eating out of my hand before you could have said ''Mary Baker Eddy.'' Now come on, start mooing.

ESMÉ   Start what?

NOËL	Mooing. Alf Dixon's exercises are wonderful. I'm as clear as a bell this morning and am going to make a *triumphant* last appearance. (*he moos up and down the scale*)
ESMÉ	(*shuddering*) I am thankful to say I have my own methods for unseeing error.

NOËL *puts some comic wobbles into his moo and* ESMÉ *giggles.*

	You really are a fiend, Poj! That's just what you've always done. Made me absolutely infuriated with you, and then done something totally idiotic.
NOËL	I know. I'm impossibly frivolous. Now what about some bacon and . . . Would you like a nice fresh sunnyside-up egg?
ESMÉ	No, thank you. (*looking at plate*) What *am* I doing with this? I don't *want* a bun.
NOËL	You must have something.
ESMÉ	Some weak coffee, then, and a small piece of toast.
NOËL	Would a kipper be error?
ESMÉ	It would, particularly to the kipper. It's appallingly cold in here.
NOËL	It's the unit. Think positively. The waiter has just read it the Scientific Statement of Being.

They eat and sip for a few moments, NOËL *obviously bursting for more details.*

	God! I wish I'd been there!
ESMÉ	(*grimly*) I'm sure you do.
NOËL	(*cautiously*) Were there . . . trumpets?
ESMÉ	A great many.
NOËL	Garlands? I believe they rather go for garlands when they have top personalities.
ESMÉ	There was no lack of garlands.
NOËL	What about the band? Did it play?
ESMÉ	My ears are still ringing.
NOËL	Encouraging tunes?
ESMÉ	Probably, if you happened to be going into one of history's bloodier battles.

NOËL   They *did* do you well. What about cheer-leaders?

ESMÉ   What about them? What *are* cheer-leaders?

NOËL   A kind of chorus line, *pour encourager les autres*.

ESMÉ   I thought it *was* a chorus. It seemed most out of place, even there. They were nearly naked except for pink top hats and very high-heeled boots.

NOËL   (*relishing*) And then you stood at the rostrum, all bedecked with flowers, opened your mouth — and croaked?

ESMÉ   I can deny you *that* satisfaction. When I took in the full horror of the situation I naturally told Orson that he was to return me to the hotel immediately.

NOËL   How very unprofessional of you. The show should always go on.

ESMÉ   Doubtless it did. But not with me.

NOËL   *What* a shame. They'd have loved you when you got going. They really dig the denunciatory stuff, and deep down in you, my chick, there is a healthy respect for hell-fire.

ESMÉ   That, I am afraid, is what *you* need to cultivate.

NOËL   How did Orson cope?

ESMÉ   Masterfully. He addressed them himself, saying that this time I was prepared only to make an appearance, but that I would return to speak to them at their next meeting.

NOËL   Splendid! I shall fly over especially.

ESMÉ   You must be out of your mind.

NOËL   Oh, come on, darling! You must admit it was all pretty hilarious.

ESMÉ   It was a nightmare! I had to go straight to bed to recover. I fell into *tortured* sleep.

NOËL   You've always taken things big, duckie.

ESMÉ   I have never been plunged into a situation comparable to last night.

NOËL   You'll laugh later. You always do. That's why I know there's still hope.

ESMÉ   I shall probably *knife* you later if you play any more tricks like that. It was like plunging back to 1914.

NOËL   I didn't realize the Tabithas actually joined battle. *What* a night to remember!

ESMÉ	I don't mean the war, I mean the absurd pranks you got up to when we were children.
NOËL	(*sighing*) Since you turned up yesterday I have been swamped by waves of nostalgia — (*remembering*) when I haven't been swamped by waves of hurt and fury. Do you remember . . . ?
ESMÉ	I always remember.
NOËL	. . . when you and Lynden and I dressed up as cockneys, he and I in chokers, you looking like a coster girl, and taking the tube from Victoria to Whitechapel . . .
ESMÉ	Aldgate.
NOËL	. . . chiacking the passengers . . .
ESMÉ	Why they didn't rise as one and slay us, I shall never know. You made remarks about some of them that were scurrilous to the point of obscene libel.
NOËL	They loved it. They thought us real Cockney characters.
ESMÉ	I suppose it was all part of our training.
NOËL	(*nostalgically*) And tying the knockers of adjoining houses so that neither door could be opened . . .
ESMÉ	*That* didn't train us for much, but I agree it was fun at the time.
NOËL	It was *all* fun at the time. Even our arguments. God, how we argued!
ESMÉ	In those days you were capable of thinking.
NOËL	You didn't enjoy a monopoly.
ESMÉ	Yours was the sharper mind, but mine had the depth and continuity.
NOËL	I'm not going to rise. We made good foils for each other.
ESMÉ	It wouldn't have worked unless you had had an intense desire for knowledge. And you *did*, then. If only you hadn't let it submerge . . .
NOËL	Now, now, duckie . . .

The 'phone rings. NOËL *answers it.*

	Yes? . . . Who? . . . (*puts hand over receiver*) It can't be! The desk say Aubrey Carruthers is downstairs.
ESMÉ	Good heavens! And you can *jeer* at *déjà vu*!
NOËL	I never have. She's a dear old thing. (*into 'phone*) Is he short

but idiotically good-look . . . ? Never mind. You'd better send him up.

ESMÉ (*going to mirror*) He must be sixty if he's a day.

NOËL (*joining her*) Little men always wear well.

ESMÉ He was dapper more than little.

NOËL He was little. Tiny. Bumptious, but tiny. Lynden used to say his head was too near his bottom.

ESMÉ Lynden said that of any man who wasn't a towering six foot two. Anyway, he was charming, not bumptious, and he wasn't much shorter than you. Because his *brain* wasn't as sharp as yours, you have come to think of him as short in stature.

NOËL (*preening*) I agree he was charming, but he was bumptious as well.

ESMÉ You were one to talk.

NOËL I was precocious, not bumptious.

ESMÉ You should have heard what Hawtrey called you.

NOËL I did. Frequently. I still loved him.

ESMÉ Is Aubrey alone?

NOËL It seems so.

ESMÉ There must have been a wife by now.

NOËL Not necessarily. It may be a Marine sergeant.

ESMÉ Look at my nose! It's like a good deed. I must use your bathroom.

NOËL If he is interested in either of our noses, it will be mine.

ESMÉ *exits;* NOËL *follows. After a short interval the door bell rings.* NOËL *reappears in a more becoming dressing gown, smoothing his hair, and goes to door. The man who enters has luxuriant, well-styled grey hair, and remarkably preserved features. Although not tall, he has an excellent figure. His dark blue blazer sports a crisp white handkerchief and a red rose. His voice is languid and very English, inclining to the "orf" and "gawn" style. He looks ten years younger than Noel.*

AUBREY (*on the threshold*) My dear Noël, what an age it has been! (*he enters*)

NOËL   (*shaking his hand*) Thirty-five years if a day.

AUBREY   I'd have known you anywhere.

NOËL   You look precisely the same. My dear Aubrey, this is unbelievable. You were being remembered only yesterday. It just shows the power of E.S.P.

AUBREY   (*noticing the trolley*) But I'm interrupting your breakfast.

NOËL   Not at all. We're disgracefully late, but finished.

AUBREY   Oh, I didn't realize . . .

NOËL   No, no, you won't guess who's here too. You remember *Charley's Aunt*?

AUBREY   Of course I do. Like yesterday.

NOËL   And Esmé Wynne? Stoj?

AUBREY   Vividly. A pretty little thing, and so clever. I've often wondered what happened to her.

NOËL   She turned up yesterday. (*he pushes trolley into lobby*)

AUBREY   How extraordinary! And like you, I suppose — not changed one iota.

NOËL   On the contrary, she has changed like anything. She has made a point of it. She is totally hooked on the spiritual side of things and has gone from strength to strength, with purity oozing from every pore.

AUBREY   Dear Stoj. Such a talented little actress, but perhaps a shade out of touch with reality.

NOËL   I think she took time to realize that the world is antagonistic to those of special susceptibilities.

ESMÉ *enters.*

          Darling! You look *transformed.*

ESMÉ   Don't be ridiculous, Poj.

She sweeps past him and has a full centre-stage reunion with Aubrey — the outstretched arms, the feet together, the head thrown back enough to flatten the chins and add an edge of provocation to the eyes.

          Aubrey, my dear, I would have known you anywhere.

NOËL   That line is already a little faded.

AUBREY   My dear, dear Stoj! (*regarding her at arms' length*) Noël and I
          were just agreeing it is thirty-five years. We must have
          hopelessly miscalculated.

ESMÉ   You must indeed. I have given up trying to make Noël more
          metaphysical about time.

AUBREY   (*kissing her hand*) May you forever stay living proof of time's
          false witness.

NOËL   What a gruesome idea.

ESMÉ   Aubrey, if you flirt with me on *that* level I shall fall hopelessly
          in love with you.

NOËL   Before this gets out of hand, what can I offer you, Aubrey?
          Would some champagne seem too dreadfully . . . ?

AUBREY   Bless you, I never do these days. There were some warning
          signs a few years ago, and I find it better not to poison the
          system. I try to keep it in tune to cope with life's endless
          challenge.

NOËL   How strange! That's precisely why I poison it.

ESMÉ   Well, your motives may not have been the highest, Aubrey
          dear, but the result is wonderful.

AUBREY   How kind you are. For quite a while I was under a natural
          hygienist.

NOËL   How exciting! Was he attractive?

AUBREY   Noël, you're impossible! His slogan has been a constant
          inspiration: "Strength means purity, and purity starts within."

NOËL   I can see we are in for a meeting of twin minds. Perhaps I had
          better leave you alone.

ESMÉ   Poj, do stop being flippant for a moment. What have you been
          doing with yourself all these years, Aubrey darling?

NOËL   The theatre missed you.

AUBREY   I went to Hollywood for a time. Nothing terribly exciting. Then
          a few stage parts.

ESMÉ   With that profile, you were *meant* for the theatre.

NOËL   I am sure Mrs Eddy wouldn't approve of this obsession with
          the outward.

AUBREY   (*showing his profile and conscious of the mirror*) As a matter of
          fact, one of my greatest successes was in *Present Laughter*.

ESMÉ   Noël sent me the text. I *read* it. I can just see you as . . . what was his name? . . . Garry! Garry Essendine. So where . . . ?

AUBREY (*hastily*) Anyway, I am afraid marriage then caught up with me.

ESMÉ Why "afraid"?

AUBREY Well, it seems to have happened rather often. Marriage, I mean.

NOËL Perfectly understandable. A waste, but perfectly understandable.

AUBREY (*pathetically*) I don't know what it is about me, but I always seem to attract the same kind of woman, if you know what I mean.

ESMÉ Warm and protective?

AUBREY More . . . forceful.

ESMÉ (*stoutly*) I am sure any normal, nice type of woman would want to marry you. They obviously respond to a very desirable quality in the essential you.

AUBREY (*gloomily*) My last one admitted it was my money. She took a lot of it away with her.

ESMÉ I am sure there was much more to it than that.

AUBREY Anyway, enough about me. (*to* NOËL) What a wonderful success you have had here. I have been away, so haven't actually seen the show, but I know the reception has been tremendous.

NOËL (*modestly*) People have been most responsive.

AUBREY I'm delighted for you, absolutely delighted.

NOËL Yes, the lull was getting rather depressing.

AUBREY Lull?

ESMÉ When his public had . . . well, gone off the boil a little.

AUBREY Gone off the boil?

NOËL Gawn orf the boil. It does happen.

AUBREY Yes, well, that rather brings me to my reason for calling on you. Well, part of the reason. (*he looks embarrassed*) I feel slightly guilty.

NOËL I am sure you have no need.

AUBREY I think the name Patti Logan may ring a bell for you . . . ?

NOËL Frequent bells. She keeps on 'phoning me.

ESMÉ She's apparently one of these women who collect personalities the way pony children seek rosettes.

NOËL	Her husband has money in my show.
AUBREY	That was her last husband. She still uses his name professionally.
NOËL	And who's the current victim? No, don't tell me!
AUBREY	(*nodding*) Yes.
NOËL	My dear Aubrey! The warmest congratulations!
ESMÉ	There is quite obviously a *lot* of good in her.
AUBREY	Patti is very go-ahead. Full of ideas.
NOËL	My impression entirely. Do you really like being married to bossy women, Aubrey?
AUBREY	A lot gets taken off one's hands.
NOËL	Including one's capital, I imagine.
AUBREY	She's not too bad if you stand up to her.
ESMÉ	*Do* you stand up to her?
AUBREY	It's difficult. She doesn't listen very much.
NOËL	(*to* ESMÉ) Only like you do, darling — with the aim of contradiction and the vain hope of reform. So whose money is in my show — yours or Logan's?
AUBREY	Logan's, I suppose.
NOËL	Only ''suppose''?
AUBREY	(*gesturing*) Things are a little complicated. I met Patti through doing business with him, just as they were breaking up. You know how quickly things happen over here. But he's more of a property man. She . . . we . . . have gone into promotion — mostly of theatre and film people, do you see. Patti has big schemes.
NOËL	Your money, her ideas?
AUBREY	That was the general plan.
NOËL	So she sent you up here to . . . pave the way?
ESMÉ	Oh, but I wanted to see you in any case — of course.
NOËL	Of course.
AUBREY	*She'd* better explain. I shall get it wrong.
NOËL	Is she here?
AUBREY	Having a coffee in the lounge.
NOËL	My dear Aubrey, I don't know what to say. So far from feeling in the mood to be promoted any more, I am rather looking forward to a spell of serene incognito in dear old London

AUBREY   Of course. You must be exhausted after all this. But we are
         going . . . well, international, do you see?

The 'phone rings. NOËL *answers it.*

NOËL   Coley! My poppet! How wonderful to hear your voice
         again! . . . Yes, you still sound a little as though you would
         a-wooing go. What does the doctor say? . . . Tomorrow!
         That's marvellous news! So it wasn't flu after all, then? . . .
         Well, there you are, duckie, that doughty old divine Mind has
         been at it again . . . Oh, everything's fine on the impurely
         material level. Just a dressing gown needing a clever mend.
         Look, dearie, hold on a minute while I take this 'phone into
         the bedroom. Another old friend has just turned up and is
         here with Stoj, and I know they want to let their hair down.

He unplugs the 'phone and takes it into bedroom.

         (*as he exits*) Now you can get down to the things that really
         matter.
AUBREY   He hasn't changed a great deal, has he?
ESMÉ   No more mentally than you have physically, alas.
AUBREY   (*sentimentally*) But auld lang syne still counts for much.
ESMÉ   There's no other explanation.
AUBREY   But what are *you* doing in Vegas? I thought you left the stage
         and became a writer.
ESMÉ   (*gently reproving*) I was always a writer, Aubrey.
AUBREY   Yes, of course, my dear, you did everything divinely well. But
         didn't you turn rather . . . religious?
ESMÉ   What was always deep within me has simply evolved over
         the years.
AUBREY   It's a dreadful admission to have to make, but I don't believe
         I have ever actually read one of your books.
ESMÉ   I must give you a copy of my latest. It is the quintessence of
         my life's quest for spiritual Truth. I doubt if I shall ever have
         anything more important to give to the world.
AUBREY   My dearest Stoj, it will have my undivided attention. But how
         sad that you gave up the stage.

ESMÉ   Aubrey, my dear, we must all be prepared to be led. I was led to leave the stage. It is wrong to outline. There is only one Will, and life's true secret is to submit to the dictates of a higher Power.

AUBREY   I think that is what most of my wives have been at pains to impress upon me.

ESMÉ   (*laughing*) My poor Aubrey!

AUBREY   I sometimes suspect I may rather have . . . well, squandered my life.

ESMÉ   Perhaps you will be shown how to make up for it now you have matured. I know I have.

AUBREY   No really worthwhile opportunity seems to have turned up.

ESMÉ   Have you thought of promoting ideas rather than people?

AUBREY   It would be so difficult. People are much more interested in people than in ideas.

ESMÉ   I know. You see them in zoos, looking at monkeys. There is very little to choose between them. But if you promoted the right ideas, Aubrey, you would be helping people to find a greater satisfaction than absorption in personality.

AUBREY   (*a little out of depth*) I'm sure you're right, Stoj dear, but I think Patti would take a lot of convincing.

ESMÉ   Do you *live* in this awful place?

AUBREY   Only recently. Patti has a house in a suburb called Paradise, do you see, and she feels Vegas is a good centre for our work.

NOËL *re-enters with 'phone and reconnects it. He has changed into a jacket.*

NOËL   Sorry, darlings, I just had to have a few moments with dear Coley. He's going to be up and about again tomorrow.

ESMÉ   How extraordinary this all is. It's almost as though we were being shown.

AUBREY   Shown?

ESMÉ   By Mind.

NOËL   I expect he's a little behind you, darling. If something has been *shown*, Aubrey, it is almost certainly *meant*. Once you have grasped that elementary fact, all is made clear.

AUBREY	(*at sea*) Ah, yes!
ESMÉ	Nothing happens by chance. We are all brought together for a purpose.
NOËL	Maybe I am getting metaphysical in my old age, but do you know I have been to parties the world over where even *I* have had my doubts about that?
ESMÉ	Persistent pursuit of the trivial must, of course, temporarily interrupt the evolutionary process.
NOËL	You see how she's come on, Aubrey? But underneath she hasn't changed a bit.
AUBREY	(*gushingly*) Would we want her otherwise, bless her?
NOËL	What fools men are.
ESMÉ	I think *Aubrey* knows what it is to feel in need of a sense of direction.
NOËL	Stoj is on a lecture tour. Teaching the natives their true priorities. They're lapping it up.
AUBREY	You really are a wonder, Stoj darling. I wish I had a tenth of your brains.
NOËL	It's all a far, far cry from *Charley's Aunt*.
AUBREY	My word, yes!
NOËL	That bitter spring of 1916 . . .
ESMÉ	Winter. We opened on January 31st.
NOËL	In Blackpool.
ESMÉ	At the Marlborough. In London.
AUBREY	Stoj is right.
NOËL	Do you remember dear old James Page?
ESMÉ	Permanently squiffy.
NOËL	He lost his teeth in the kedgeree in Manchester.
ESMÉ	Bolton. Do you remember that song I wrote for your birthday party, Aubrey?
NOËL	With my music.
AUBREY	Of course.
NOËL	How did it go?

He goes to piano.

ESMÉ	We made it up as we went along. The usual way.

NOËL   I wonder if we still could?

He pauses a moment then begins to pick out a tune. When he speaks, he is feeling his way into a lyric, and ESMÉ *responds.*

There was a day — do you remember? — It was . . . oh, in late July . . .

ESMÉ   No, early June.

NOËL   For all I know, it could have been September . . .

ESMÉ   It doesn't matter. Focus on the tune.

NOËL   How did it go?

ESMÉ   *(after hesitation, gesturing)* Dum, dum — *dum* de dum.

NOËL   *(recalling)* Dum, dum — de *dum* de dum.

ESMÉ   Something like that. We waltzed to it.

AUBREY   ''Little . . .''?

NOËL   *(nodding)* ''Little girl I love,
                      Tell me you love me too.''

ESMÉ   ''Little boy I love,
                 That I shall always do.''

BOTH   ''Little girl/boy I love,
                 Tell me you love me too.
                 Stars in the sky above,
                 They know that I love you.''

NOËL   The saints preserve us!

He plays a few more notes.

''Of all the things our elders say
                 To shield us from the awful day
                 When love wins through,
                 The silliest that comes to mind
                 Is the one that love is blind —
                 And yet . . . it's awfully true.''

ESMÉ   Because . . . ?

NOËL   Because *(now inventing)* . . . I didn't even like you, that fatal day we met . . .

ESMÉ   You told me that I bleated! Of all the cheek!

NOËL   And yet . . . There was a certain something in the way you
          held your head . . .
ESMÉ   I could tell that you had noticed because your ears turned red.
NOËL   ''I never knew I'd know you as you are.''
          You wrote a ghastly poem about the great god Pan . . .
ESMÉ   And then you made me giggle in the way you always can.
BOTH   ''I never knew I'd know you as you are.''
NOËL   I wonder how it happened?
ESMÉ   We just grew on one another.
NOËL   Like adolescent acne . . .
ESMÉ   Or a sister. . .
NOËL   Or a brother.
ALL   ''And now at last I see you as you are.''

          ESMÉ *and* AUBREY *begin to waltz.*

          ''Little girl/boy I love,
            Tell me you love me too.
            Little girl/boy I love,
            That I shall always do.

            Little girl/boy I love,
            Tell me you love me too.
            Stars in the sky above,
            They know that I love you.''

NOËL   (*dropping his hands in his lap*) Oh, dear!
AUBREY   We all have to start somewhere.
ESMÉ   Well at least it was as clean as a whistle.

          They laugh.

          Door bell rings.

NOËL   I have known people who have asked me in all seriousness
          how I cope with being alone.
AUBREY   Oh, dear, I am afraid it may be Patti. Perhaps I should let her in.

NOËL   I am sure you should.

> AUBREY *goes to door and opens it.* PATTI LOGAN *enters. She is in early middle age, slim and good-looking in a metallic, immaculate way. Any slight over-statement in her expensive clothes and accessories lacks overt vulgarity. This conscious restraint is also, at least initially, in her manner, which belies the hard mouth and eyes. Her southern-tinged, rather wheedling voice only partly hides the steel beneath. At first glance she might make a good President's wife, but whatever her ambitions may be, we detect below the sophisticated exterior a parochial core.*

PATTI   (*steel uppermost*) You were coming down for me, Aubrey.
AUBREY   I know, Patti, I'm so very sorry. It has been a triple reunion and then Noël had to take a 'phone call.
PATTI   You could have rung down.
AUBREY   But . . .
NOËL   (*coming forward*) My dear Mrs Logan! At last!
PATTI   I sure wish it could have been sooner, Mr Coward.
NOËL   The waiting has merely sharpened the final pleasure. May I introduce Esmé Wynne-Tyson?
ESMÉ   (*shaking hands*) How do you do?
PATTI   (*disinterest poorly disguised*) My pleasure.
NOËL   Can I get you something to drink, Mrs Logan?
PATTI   Nothing, thank you. (*for* AUBREY's *benefit*) I have coffee running out of my ears.
NOËL   How beastly for you.

> ESMÉ *goes into* NOËL's *bedroom.*

AUBREY   I said I was sorry, my dear.
PATTI   (*trying to show charm*) Anyway, it is very gracious of you to see us, Mr Coward.
NOËL   It was the least I could do. I am so grateful for your contribution to my appearance in Vegas.
PATTI   I'm real glad it has been such a triumph, Mr Coward.
NOËL   You must call me Noël.

PATTI   They all know me as Patti.

ESMÉ re-enters holding NOËL's *dressing gown and a mending kit.
She puts on glasses and begins to sew.*

Now, I must tell you, Noël, I can't forgive myself or Logan
for letting you stay in this crummy hotel. But I've had to be
in Memphis and going around a lot, and since Logan and I
split up — like you may have heard — I've had no hand in
his arrangements.

NOËL   Everyone has done their best to make me feel at home.

PATTI   No hotel's a home, Noël. That's why I — that is, Aubrey and
me — we'd be so happy for you to visit with us. We have a
very comfortable house in the best part of Paradise.

NOËL   It sounds heavenly.

PATTI   (*nodding*) It's real nice. Pool, tennis court, resident masseuse
["masooz"] — and my chef . . . well, he was thirty years in
Paris, France. Need I say more?

NOËL   Indeed you needn't. The mouth waters.

PATTI   Now I sure am sad you mean to return to England so soon
after being sick. Will you let me persuade you to join Aubrey
and me just for a week so as to get yourself back on your feet
and real fit? I'd just love for you to see our home and meet
my daughter Claudine.

AUBREY   We could take you for some quite charming drives.

PATTI   That's right, and really set you up again.

NOËL   You're immensely kind, but everything seems to be pushing
me into a quick return to London.

PATTI   That's a real shame. I'm sure there are so many very lovely
people who would just be crazy to meet you after your great
reception here.

NOËL   No one should ever under-estimate the intensity of American
hospitality.

PATTI   I hope you will always look back on your time in Vegas and
feel we made a real contribution to your return to popularity.

ESMÉ   He is still a little remembered back home.

AUBREY   Of course, of course.

NOËL	But my time here has been most heartening, it truly has.
PATTI	Still, you know what they say about one swallow not making a summer.
NOËL	It's very true, of course.
PATTI	Right. And old balls don't bounce so high, neither.
NOËL	Not only true, but colourful.
PATTI	One has to be realistic in this hard world, Noël.
NOËL	Indeed one does, Patti.
PATTI	Have you anything . . . well, real meaningful to get back to in London?
NOËL	Oh, yes, quite a lot, one way or another.
PATTI	It's great the way things are picking up for you. Mind, you had quite a hit with some film way back, didn't you?
NOËL	There has been the odd modest success.
AUBREY	Patti has not had much to do with the British scene, I am afraid, Noël.
PATTI	One can't be into everything, Aubrey.
AUBREY	Noël has done a great deal before he came to Vegas, Patti.
PATTI	Do you think I don't know that, Aubrey? Why, there was that play he had on Broadway last year.
AUBREY	With the Lunts! That's all! On Broadway!
PATTI	All I'm saying is, no one can sit back and take things for granted these days.
NOËL	That is absolutely true.
PATTI	Which is why I hope Aubrey has told you a little about our plans.
NOËL	Only some fragments. We were diverted by nostalgia.
PATTI	We are going . . . (*she pauses impressively*) international.
NOËL	My word! I'm sure you'll do wonderfully well.
PATTI	(*nodding*) I mean we shall.
NOËL	Everything, in my experience, boils down to the power of mind. Wouldn't you agree, Stoj?

ESMÉ *looks at him.*

PATTI	So may I level with you, Noël?
NOËL	It is always best in the long run, Patti.
PATTI	Like I said, I guess it's no secret you've been through a bad stretch. Work-wise, I mean.

NOËL   The graph certainly did level out a bit. Something to do with
           the kitchen-sink school, they say.

PATTI   Well, Vegas should have helped change all that.

NOËL   (*patiently*) I'm immensely grateful. I do hope you understand
           that.

           ESMÉ's *eyes turn to ceiling.*

PATTI   O.K. But like I said — one swallow . . .

NOËL   (*nodding*) And those leaden balls.

PATTI   So Aubrey and I, we'd like to help that change along.

NOËL   It's most kind of you.

PATTI   Time was, people'd think it enough to go for the little things
           — you know, face-lifts and a snip here and there — but today
           it's basically a matter of image and projection.

NOËL   I am sure it is.

PATTI   By the way, I know someone who can do a lift real cheap.
           Nice neat job and no come-back.

NOËL   There you are, Stoj. As you've always said, wait to be shown,
           don't outline, and it's plonked on your lap.

PATTI   You see, Noël, we're into the era of the personality. The time's
           gone when it was enough just to write a book or a play and
           then sit back and let others put it over.

NOËL   None of us can escape the marketplace.

PATTI   That's right, Noël, and as we get older we don't have the same
           energy any more.

NOËL   The barrow-boy needs more than his grapefruits.

PATTI   (*nodding*) Right. A man in his mature years cannot be expected
           to write works of genius *and* go out and sell them.

NOËL   Diversify or perish.

PATTI   The personal image — *that's* what matters. That's why it was
           such a pity about Gertrude Lawrence.

NOËL   A pity?

PATTI   Her dying like that.

NOËL   Yes, indeed. I felt it keenly. I was devoted to Gertie. Aubrey
           will remember.

AUBREY   Yes, yes, she was a great asset to the theatre — once they tidied
           her up a little.

PATTI	Devoted. Exactly. And that is what you lack, Noël. An object for your devotion. (*she pauses*) You are a man alone.
NOËL	I am so seldom conscious of it.
PATTI	Even so, a man alone is a man halved in his selling power. Women see that more clearly than most men.
NOËL	I am sure they do. It's a most perceptive sex.
PATTI	Now if you were still with Gertrude . . .
NOËL	Gertie. She was always Gertie.
PATTI	Gertie, then. If she was still around, we could have gone places for you.
NOËL	We?
PATTI	Aubrey and me.
NOËL	I think I'm being a little dense.
PATTI	We would have sold the ta*bleaux* of you and Gertie together. Inseparable.
NOËL	Just to clarify one little point once for all, we were never together in the biblical sense.
PATTI	(*seriously*) You've got to be seen to have a relationship, Noël. That's today's message.
NOËL	It is not easy keeping up with today's messages.
PATTI	What's more, if you've something to sell — in the creative, artistic world, that is — that relationship has got to be made to work for you. That right, Aubrey?
AUBREY	Undoubtedly.
NOËL	I suppose there is much to be said for the slippers and pipe at the end of a hard day.
PATTI	(*with rather chilling roguishness*) Now, Noël, you are not really as innocent as all that!
NOËL	No, I must admit that of all the charges I have had levelled at me, particularly in the last twenty-four hours, innocence was not one of them.
PATTI	Then we both know that if Gertie was still alive you could have been seen to have a relationship that would have kept the world at your feet. You know that young actress Elizabeth Taylor?
AUBREY	A pretty child.
NOËL	A girl on her way up, from all accounts.
PATTI	And for why? Because she understands the power of relation-

ships. Of publicity.

NOËL   I am old fashioned, I'm sure, but I believe the product is more important in the long run than the gift-wrapping.

PATTI   O.K., there's maybe a danger she'll make her name through her marriages rather than from acting, but she's learning all the time.

NOËL   The virus has affected my faculties — what is the connection with Gertie?

PATTI   Like I said, with Aubrey and me around, you and Gertie would have had an on-going relationship that kept the world on its toes.

NOËL   My dear Patti, it was very on-going. At her best, Gertie was a great artiste. Her role in *Private Lives* will go down in theatrical history.

PATTI   Sure, sure! But as of now, if we'd been handling things you'd be a towering, tragic hulk of a man, ravaged and near destroyed by your loss.

NOËL   I don't know that I want to be a towering, tragic hulk. It sounds rather uninviting.

PATTI   I mean broken up by the loss of someone your heart could never replace.

NOËL   The show has to go on.

PATTI   No question. But don't miss my point, Noël. Today's public looks for more than a working relationship.

NOËL   Then the world must make do with what it is given. An awful lot of nonsense has been talked about my friendship with Gertie, and doubtless much more is on the horizon. But believe me — for all that she sang ''Parisian Pierrot'' divinely and may have been associated in the public mind with a languid nostalgia for the camp and effete, she had a robust personal preference for the butchier Guards officers. A thin red line was almost permanently in tow.

PATTI   It's what the public's told that matters.

NOËL   (*repressing impatience*) But my dear Mrs . . . Patti, Gertie is dead and gone, and I assure you that neither Liz Taylor nor I have anything under wraps. Not as between ourselves, anyway.

PATTI   I wasn't planning anything for the Taylor girl.

NOËL   That at least is a relief.

ESMÉ   I can't believe it is necessary to go to such lengths. My publisher attends to my books' publicity.

PATTI   It's not enough, dear.

NOËL   I think Patti has in mind something juicier than the kind of thing the Orson Humdingers of this world can lay on.

PATTI   (*short laugh*) *That* beat up old faggot! He's in town right this moment, pushing some dowdy little English woman who's on some kind of religious circuit. That's about all he's good for. Poor thing, she must be on her last legs to have *him* handle her.

AUBREY *looks enquiringly at* NOËL. NOËL *nods. They cover their eyes.* ESMÉ *jabs needle into couch.*

NOËL   So where does this get us, Patti? For different reasons, Liz Taylor and Gertie can play no part in your scheme of things.

PATTI   No problem. I've someone in mind. She's young, attractive, an excellent actress.

NOËL   If there is one thing I have never been short of, it is young, attractive actresses. Every time I write a play, I am swamped by shoals of young, attractive actresses.

PATTI   (*patiently*) See here, Noël, all you have to do is write a part for her, be seen around, feed a few rumours, get photographed in the right places . . . all that stuff. Aubrey and I will fix everything.

AUBREY   Patti, my dear, I do think this may not be quite the approach to find favour with Noël.

PATTI   Now, Aubrey, just leave me to know my business.

AUBREY   (*to* NOËL) You might not believe it, but there is still a strange quality of innocence about Patti.

NOËL   Of course I believe you. The testimony of the material senses, as Stoj knows so well, is often fallible.

PATTI   The first thing is for you to meet her. I can get her over this evening.

NOËL   Meet who?

PATTI   My daughter, Claudine.

NOËL	Your daughter is the attractive young actress who is to take the place — more than the place — of Gertie in my life?
PATTI	That's how I see it, Noël. Or how the world will see it.
NOËL	My dear Patti, with the greatest possible respect for your inventiveness, enthusiasm and disinterested concern with my future, I think you must be just a teeny bit round the bend.
AUBREY	I did tell you, Patti . . .
NOËL	You want me to take up — outwardly, at least — with the daughter by your marriage to Mr Logan?
PATTI	She's my first husband's child, not Logan's.
NOËL	Forgive my insensitivity.
PATTI	When you meet her, I figure the whole scenario will grab you. She's a very lovely girl. Very talented. She'd go along with the whole idea.
AUBREY	Patti, there are all sorts of reasons why Noël can't be interested in this sort of approach.
PATTI	I am sure — *thank* you, Aubrey (*glaring*) — that Noël is a man to put his career before everything.
NOËL	Not quite everything. You see, I do already have a "relationship".

ESMÉ *holds dressing gown up to light to examine her work on it.* PATTI *looks at her.*

ESMÉ	(*casually, as though no one else was present*) The temperature in here has become quite pleasant again, hasn't it, Poj?
PATTI	You mean you are married already?
NOËL	Not married exactly, no . . .
AUBREY	But someone very dear to you?
NOËL	Very dear. Both of them.
PATTI	Both?
NOËL	Yes. My family.
PATTI	I never heard you had a family.
NOËL	Coley and Graham are my family.
PATTI	You got sons?
NOËL	Not sons. Very dear friends and workmates I choose to live with.

PATTI   It's not the same though, is it?

NOËL   It's good enough for me. A relationship doesn't only consist of bouncing about in bed night after night.

ESMÉ   Really, Mrs Logan, you don't seem to know anything at all about Noël. Why are you wasting his time with these extraordinary and distasteful suggestions?

PATTI   (*offended*) I am sure that all I am concerned for is that dear Noël here should see his great reputation revived and sustained. That's all we have been discussing.

ESMÉ   He is quite capable of recovering his reputation without descending to the silly tricks you've outlined.

PATTI   This side of the water, my dear, fame doesn't come that easy.

ESMÉ   This side of the water, I suspect, fame may not be worth what it takes to achieve it.

PATTI   But we're agreed we all want the best for Noël?

ESMÉ   I have wanted the best for Noël all my life. He has never shown the slightest interest in possessing it. What *you* appear to want for him is more and more of what has made him what he is today.

PATTI   That's right, dear. A great man with a great potential.

ESMÉ   A *worldly* success.

PATTI   I see no reason to sneer at worldly success.

ESMÉ   In that respect at least you have something in common with poor Noël.

PATTI   It's in his own interests to make the top of the heap.

ESMÉ   You make him sound like a dung-beetle. And that's what you regard as the "best" for Noël — financial profit and regular headlines in the tabloids?

PATTI   You'd prefer he hit poverty level? Become a Broadway bum?

NOËL   (*slumping into chair*) Look, dears, I think it best you both accept you have rather different angles on life. I have a busy evening ahead and really should rest my voice.

PATTI   If you had the right *woman*, Noël, so much could be taken off your shoulders.

NOËL   After a lifetime of closely scrutinizing my friends' private lives, I am utterly unconvinced that involvement with the opposite sex will reduce one's burden.

AUBREY   Really, Patti, you *are* making rather an ass of yourself. Surely
          you can accept that Noël is just not interested in emotional
          involvement with a woman. Not even if simulated. We need
          a different approach.

PATTI   Whether or not Claudine gotten involved, it's only the pro-
          jection we have to worry about. I'm just trying to establish
          the principle.

ESMÉ   Principle!

PATTI   A better known actress, someone a little more mature, might
          be even better. I'm flexible.

NOËL   But I don't really think *I* am. You may mean well, Patti, but
          I am a shade long in the tooth to change my ways to suit the
          world's voyeuristic appetite. I think I'll just have to muddle
          on writing my plays and tossing off the occasional trivial song,
          the only way I understand. I know neither you nor Esmé —
          for somewhat different reasons — feels that is enough, but
          I fear you must both learn to live with it.

PATTI   It really bugs me to see people squander their potential.

NOËL   Esmé would say much the same.

Door bell rings.

          (*wearily*) Pray God it is a waiter laden with poisons or darling
          Coley early returned to the fold. (*he goes to door and opens it*)
          Oh, no, this is too much!

*The young woman who enters has a round, anxious face, made more
earnest by the large round spectacles she wears. Her hair suggests
that appearance is not a priority.*

MABEL   You remember me, Mr Coward? Mabel Thrift of the Courier.

NOËL   I remember you vividly, Mabel. I also remember very distinctly
          telling you that I did not wish to be interviewed again.

MABEL   I know that, Mr Coward. That's why I've come. I felt real
          terrible about last time. I just talked about me. I figured that
          when I saw how little I'd gotten on to my writing block. I want
          you to know I think I'm figuring things out now. I think

they're coming straight. This morning I woke up and I wasn't
hating my mother like I did.

NOËL   I'm delighted, Mabel, but this really isn't the time or place
to talk it through.

MABEL   (*intensely*) I'm sorry! I'm sorry! There I go again! Look, I just
wanted to make up for it with a real in-depth confrontation
that would give the Courier's readers true insight into Mr Noël
Coward the man.

NOËL   Just at the moment, Mabel, Mr Noël Coward the man is feeling he has been put through a wringer. I woke this morning
with an irrational presentiment it was going to be one of those
days, and I was right to a tee.

ESMÉ   He's very tired, Miss Thrift.

NOËL   And very old, badly in need of a break, devoid of on-going
relationships, and rapidly sinking into the quagmire of an
unrepentant materialism. Down, damned and done for.

PATTI   Now, Noël, I didn't mean to belittle your past achievements.
You know that.

ESMÉ   Your absurd proposal to saddle him with some shallow little
floosie proves you are even more insensitive to his future.

PATTI   Claudine is a very lovely person, Esmé. You should not make
such a judgment.

AUBREY   Young women just aren't Noël's scene, Patti.

PATTI   Well, I'm mighty sorry to hear that. Without a full relationship, no man is a real person.

ESMÉ   By ''full relationship'' you mean sex.

PATTI   Sex is a very big part of life, Esmé dear.

ESMÉ   So many choose to believe. For some it becomes the weak-
ling's distraction from the path to spiritual wisdom. In any
case, Noël is a grown man who can make his own arrangements in that direction.

PATTI   Then it's a very great shame he hasn't done so. The last few
years might not have been so wasted.

ESMÉ   Have you any right to judge that Noël's last few years have
been wasted? Fulfilment is not necessarily synonymous with
having one's name permanently in lights in Shaftesbury
Avenue and on Broadway.

PATTI   All I'm saying is he'd have done better if he had had someone
. . . well, you know — special.

ESMÉ   As it happens, Noël had a very special relationship for several
years and was most upset when it came to an end. Possibly
a lot more upset, from what I have heard, than you were when
any of your own "special relationships" ended. But with a
possibly short-sighted disregard for the publicity oppor-
tunities, he did not then, and would not now, exploit it to
gratify others' appetite for cheap sensationalism and the public
washing of private linen.

MABEL   I'd sure love to talk about it, Mr Coward.

PATTI   But *I* have been married. It seems that Noël's only close
relationship has been with a man.

ESMÉ   So what point are you making? Are you suggesting that two
men are incapable of a relationship in which mental and
physical mean as much as between man and woman?

PATTI   I guess I am talking about what is natural and unnatural, Esmé.

ESMÉ   Then I suggest you have not studied life in much depth. The
norm isn't so easily pinned down. God knows — and so does
Noël — that I disapprove profoundly of homosexuality. The
fact remains that while some men and women will go with
their own sex even against their actual physical inclinations,
there are many others whose natures goad them to flout con-
vention, often to their own distress and regret. Deviance can
overwhelm wisdom.

PATTI   I have never denied that.

ESMÉ   You may never have denied it, but have you accepted it as
"natural" as readily as you would some promiscuous
heterosexual with a trail of broken marriages and unwanted
children? It is one thing to pay lip service to others' right to
be different, quite another to *feel* that right vicariously and to
understand the obligations it imposes on us. Tolerance and
love can be worlds apart. We tell ourselves that *non*-humans
— dogs, apes, and the poor beasts we perversely rear for food
— have a right to life, but we don't feel it in our hearts. We
ignore the uncomfortable fact that cruelty can't be selective,
and that we shall never behave better towards each other

until we have learned to be compassionate to creatures weaker than ourselves. We inflict on them the most appalling suffering with hope of finding cures for the consequences of our stupid way of life and because we want to eat their bodies. Our excuse is that they are a different species. Many of us see homosexuals in much the same way — something apart, something we must tolerate because they have human form, but little more deserving of our true love and compassion than some non-human who doesn't happen to share our language. Love is the only genuine basis for tolerance, Mrs Logan. Identification. Imaginative sympathy. A feeling of unity that transcends minor differences and mere physical coupling. If two people can know just one such relationship in the course of a lifetime, they are very very fortunate. The majority of us have to make do with rather less.

She has stopped sewing during this delivery and her hands are in her lap. She bites her lower lip and blinks, lowering her head a little. NOËL *rises from his chair and goes to the drinks cupboard. As he passes her he gently squeezes her shoulder.*

NOËL   I'm as weak as a kitten, I know, but I'm going to have a little something.

He pours himself a whisky, takes a sip, then turns.

Now listen, everyone, I have taken careful note of your plans and ambitions for my future, and they have convinced me that my most comforting prospect is a monotonous repetition of the past. Furthermore, this suite bears an increasing resemblance to a Cecil deMille crowd scene, and in a very short time I am supposed to be giving my final and unforgettable performance at the Desert Inn. I fear it will be an anticlimax, but even a deadbeat old trouper like me needs his brief moment of privacy and preparation. I really would be infinitely obliged if those present who have no further use for my remains would bugger off and leave me alone.

ESMÉ   (*pulling herself together*) I'll ring down for some more coffee and
            run a bath for you, then you can have a little rest. Now please,
            Mrs Logan, take Aubrey home and leave poor Noël to enjoy
            a moment's peace.

PATTI   If it's Noël's wish we should leave, then of course we will.
            But I don't see what right you have to speak to us like we were
            a bunch of kids. It's no wonder Noël switched to Gertrude
            Lawrence. He had a good instinct there.

NOËL   Esmé speaks to everyone as though they were a bunch of kids.
            Perhaps most of us are.

PATTI   Well, I'm sorry, Noël, but I don't go along with being spoken
            to like that, and I frankly don't figure what you can have seen
            in Miss Tyson here. She's not your type of person at all.

NOËL   I'll tell you what I have seen in Esmé, Patti. I have seen
            someone who really cares about me, and about this pretty
            scarey world we've made for ourselves. Oh, yes, she's bossy
            and critical and often so maddening I could fell her with the
            nearest half-brick, but if I am honest with myself — and it
            does happen from time to time — I put up with her stric-
            tures because she is basically right, has the courage to speak
            out, and devotes her life to doing so in a state of near poverty
            and almost total isolation. She could have gone right to the
            top as an actress, but instead chose a very lonely and
            materially unrewarding path for which only a tiny minority
            give her any thanks. She has said things to me I would
            forgive from no one else, but she has said them because in
            her own unique, infuriating way she really does want me
            to be a better person for my own sake and for the sake of
            a world she sees plunging into an abyss. If one day they
            sanctify dear old Stoj, I shall send a very rude letter up to
            whatever cloud she has parked her botty on, but I shan't
            be the least bit surprised at her making celestial Broadway
            and I shall open a very private bottle of champagne. Not
            that the Church *will* sanctify her, of course, because she's
            been much too rude about them and would not accept it
            anyway.

ESMÉ   But, Poj . . .

NOËL   Don't interrupt, darling, I'm beautifully into my stride. You
            see, Patti, Esmé is my oldest friend, and I can remember her
            crying bitterly at the wicked insanity of the first world war;
            I can remember her passionate desire at the ripe old age of
            twelve to know the purpose of life so that she could — poor
            deluded darling — help a world she fondly imagined would
            be eager to embrace a better pattern. Whereas the highest I
            have aimed for has been to make it laugh. She has trundled
            on evolving, as she calls it, while I have stayed practically
            stationary perfecting my talent to amuse. Mind you, I think
            it's *my* business I have chosen to do so, and I regularly and
            furiously defend my immobility whenever Esmé attacks it, but
            deep down inside me I know she's worth two of me, several
            Gerties, and at least a dozen of you. She's a marvellous party,
            and I shall love her till I die.

            ESMÉ *gets up and turns away in tears.*

PATTI   (*offended*) I'm sure I've no wish to impose myself on anyone
            who doesn't appreciate my interest in them. But I'm a mite
            surprised that a woman you say is your oldest friend, and has
            gotten some kind of religious hang-up that doesn't allow for
            sex, should come out so strong for a practice that's against
            the law of your country. I'm surprised you're happy to chance
            your . . . condition becoming common knowledge. It could
            be somewhat counter-productive, careerwise.

NOËL   I do hope, Patti, that your remark indicates concern rather than
            threat.

PATTI   If persons care to beat their breasts in front of the Press
            (*gesturing toward Mabel*), they can have no one but themselves
            to blame for the consequences.

AUBREY   Noël, my dear Stoj, this has been terribly upsetting. I really
            don't know what to say. To be quite frank with you, Patti's
            heart has been absolutely set on the possibility of handling
            Noël's promotion. Just now, it really would have meant a great
            deal to us. (*gestures*) But I do see . . . as things have turned
            out . . . Patti, I think it is time we left.

PATTI *compresses her lips and tosses her head. She and* AUBREY *go to the door.* AUBREY *holds it open for* PATTI, *and as she goes out she turns.*

PATTI   I am sorry your time in Vegas has had to end like this, Mr Coward. I daresay we shall not be seeing you over here again.

They exit.

NOËL   Life being what it is, I have often wondered why anyone bothers to write plays and novels.

ESMÉ   I'm afraid we've been terribly rude to her.

NOËL   Until today I never realized I had a mid-life identity crisis. (*pressing her arm*) You were a duck.

ESMÉ   Not really. Just telling the truth.

NOËL   I was very touched by your mention of Jack.

ESMÉ   Not by name. I'm afraid she may try to damage you.

NOËL   (*shrugs*) Tant pis. I had a little word with Coley about them. I gather Aubrey has lost all his money. I think Logan cleaned him out before thankfully unleashing Patti on to him. I was probably their last throw.

ESMÉ   Poor Aubrey! I shouldn't think it, I know, but he really might have done better if he hadn't been hetero.

NOËL   (*laughing*) I do hope Mrs Eddy didn't hear that.

MABEL, *sitting on the couch, shakes her head. She has been an agog audience throughout.*

MABEL   Gee! I don't know what to say. I just don't know what to say.

ESMÉ   You're not obliged to say anything, dear.

NOËL   I'm afraid you did rather come in at the deep end.

MABEL   My editor, he wouldn't believe it.

ESMÉ   Then perhaps you shouldn't strain his imagination. It was, after all, a rather private matter.

MABEL   (*making a guilty face*) And I wasn't even invited.

NOËL   Why not just chalk it up to experience?

ESMÉ   You could make a very interesting article — written in somewhat general terms.

MABEL   What about?

ESMÉ   Oh . . . (*gestures*), the intrusion of public relations into the
         private lives of film and theatre personalities. Something of
         a sociological piece. You look an intelligent girl.

MABEL   (*nodding*) I might do that. Kind of middle-page stuff.

ESMÉ   Exactly. With some substance to it.

MABEL   I'd like that. Road accidents, fires, muggings, that kind of stuff
         — they're not challenges any more.

NOËL   That is the trouble as one reaches maturer years.

         Mabel starts to scribble on her pad.

ESMÉ   I'd better run your bath. (*she enters bedroom*)

NOËL   (*calling*) Do you have moments, when everything is going
         wrong, of just cutting off and longing to escape?

ESMÉ   (*off*) I used to — before I found Science.

NOËL   Well, chronically lumbered with error, I still do, and right now I
         have an overwhelming longing to take the next 'plane to
         London. (*looks at watch*) There's one leaving in about two hours.

ESMÉ   But what about your final performance tonight?

NOËL   To hell with my final performance tonight.

ESMÉ   The show should always go on.

NOËL   The way my throat is feeling after all this, I doubt whether
         even a collaboration between Mrs Eddy and Alf Dixon could
         guarantee a triumphant curtain.

ESMÉ   (*entering*) But you can't just leave like that, at the drop of a hat.

NOËL   I can, you know. From what everyone's been telling me, I've
         little to lose. If Logan wanted to squeeze the last drop from
         me, he should have curbed his headhunting wife.

ESMÉ   Ex-wife. Well, I think you're being naughty, but I know that
         won't deter you.

NOËL   And do you know what I want to do as soon as I get home?

ESMÉ   Lie flat for a week, I imagine.

NOËL   I want to do what I have meant to do for years, but have never
         got round to by myself. I want to plunge right right back into
         the past in an orgy of unrepentant nostalgia, and revisit our
         old haunts — Brixton, Battersea, Clapham Common, the East
         End, the field in which we Knew, and maybe we could take

a train, preferably dodging the ticket collector, and pop down
to Lee on Solent . . .

ESMÉ   We?

NOËL *enters bedroom.*

NOËL   . . . and Lynton, where we had that ridiculous time with
Lynden on your pre-nuptial honeymoon. Do you remember
. . . ?

ESMÉ   You said ''we''.

NOËL   Well, of course I did. There'd be no fun doing it on my own.

ESMÉ   Darling, don't be absurd. I can't just rush back to England
in the middle of my lecture tour.

NOËL   You're not in the middle, and you said yourself you have
already done fifteen talks instead of the ten you'd agreed to.

ESMÉ   Even so . . .

NOËL   Think what fun it will be to have tea again at Rumplemayers
now we can really afford those ridiculously priced cakes.

ESMÉ   I'm not sure Rumplemayers survived the *first* world war, let
alone the second.

NOËL   Don't quibble, darling. There's always Fullers. We can pre-
tend. (*he enters carrying small case*)

ESMÉ   But there are all the things in my room. Some of them . . .
well, women's things.

NOËL   Coley will be up and about again tomorrow. We'll ring him
from the airport. He can pack for us both and bring the stuff
back to London. (*pinching her bottom*) He won't be a bit wor-
ried by (*darkly*) ''*women's* things''.

ESMÉ   (*half laughing*) It's an idiotic idea.

NOËL   Of course it's idiotic. That's why it's fun.

ESMÉ   I'm expected — in Baltimore and Boston.

NOËL   Bugger Baltimore and Boston. They've plenty of other
distractions.

ESMÉ   (*torn*) It has a sort of insane appeal.

NOËL   That's my Stojkins!

MABEL   (*looking up from her pad*) You're leaving?

NOËL   For dear old London Town. The pull of our old haunts and
my family are irresistible.

MABEL   (*to* ESMÉ, *sentimentally*) Oh, it was *you* all along!

ESMÉ   Me?

NOËL *takes a light coat from lobby.*

MABEL   Who has the special relationship with Mr Coward.

ESMÉ   Oh, yes, we have had a special relationship for many many years.

NOËL   (*dramatically*) One day the world may know the full story — though I expect they'll get it wrong.

MABEL   (*delighted*) Oh, that's nice! *Real* nice! Say, could I use that?

ESMÉ   Use it?

MABEL   In my paper.

ESMÉ   (*looking at* NOËL) I don't see why not.

NOËL   It will give you something of rather wider appeal. Some of the other stuff might have become a little turgid.

ESMÉ   So there you are, Mabel — an exclusive!

MABEL   Oh! Oh, that's just wonderful! (*frowning*) But what am I actually going to say?

NOËL   Just write about a very special relationship. One should never be too specific. Audiences love to be teased.

MABEL   And that's really O.K. with you?

NOËL   That's really O.K. with us.

MABEL   Gee!

NOËL   (*shaking hands with her*) Goodbye, Mabel. (*he smiles*) If this was a movie, I'd remove those spectacles, and there would be Audrey Hepburn. (*he does so.* MABEL *has a squint.* NOËL *replaces spectacles*) Anyway, it's not a movie, but just that much more improbable thing we call real life.

ESMÉ   That was almost a metaphysical statement, darling.

NOËL *holds the door open for her.*

NOËL   And Mabel, be a dear girl and 'phone Mrs Logan later to say I have had an urgent summons from the Palace.

ESMÉ   That's a fib.

NOËL   It's only a half-fib, darling. Buck House isn't the only Palace in London.

MABEL   But what about your bath?

NOËL   You have it instead, Mabel.

ESMÉ   And do something clever with your hair.

NOËL   Ring down for some more coffee.

MABEL   Gee! Really?

NOËL   Really. (*he points to the teddy bear*) And would you take over teddy? He's going to feel very lonely after the past twenty-four hours. *His* only complex is that he can't stand air travel.

The air conditioning unit springs back into life as noisily as it expired earlier. They all jump and look at it with alarm.

    (*to* MABEL) I'm afraid if you stay here long you may get very very hot.

ESMÉ   Or very very cold.

NOËL   (*to* ESMÉ) Either way, darling, our departure is quite obviously ''meant''.

They wave to MABEL *and exit.* MABEL *looks around, hugs herself, tears some pages from her pad, and begins to scribble again as*

THE CURTAIN FALLS